# EXPLORATIONS
# IN
# BASIC WRITING

## AUDREY L. REYNOLDS

Harrison Press

Printed in the United States of America.

ISBN: 978-1-58316-066-4

# EXPLORATIONS IN BASIC WRITING

To my mother and to the
memory of my father

# PREFACE

*E*xplorations in Basic Writing is designed to help students in basic or developmental writing courses to master the rules for producing good sentences in written English and, at the same time, to become familiar with some general rhetorical principles for good writing.

As the title suggests, the book is based on two fundamental premises: (1) that spoken English and written English differ in distinctive ways and (2) that students who wish to write well must learn the characteristic features of written English. For both native speakers of English and for those who are learning English as a second language, written English is a separate variety of the English language.

This book is divided into two parts. Part I, An Introduction to the Principles of Good Writing, introduces students to certain *rhetorical concepts* and some of the syntactic constructions of written English. It also gives students an opportunity to *practice* using those concepts and constructions through three kinds of exercises:

1. "Writing Workshop" exercises, which concentrate on critical reading
2. sentence-combining exercises, which focus on syntactic constructions while reinforcing rhetorical principles
3. writing assignments of two kinds—journal assignments, in which students concentrate on rhetorical principles, and composition assignments, in which students are expected to proofread in addition to applying rhetorical principles.

The *writing assignments* are designed to permit students to write about personal experience as they move from descriptive/narrative essays to expository essays. The assignments are also designed to move students one step at a time from "easy pieces," as they say in music teaching, to "hard pieces," where the relative difficulty of an assignment is determined by the complexity of the cognitive and/or rhetorical demands placed on the student.

Part II, An Introduction to the Grammar of Written English, may be used as a supplement to Part I at the instructor's discretion. Chapter 7 provides an introduction to the basic approach that will be used in Part II. The remaining chapters concentrate on *helping students learn to proofread* in order to correct various kinds of sentence-level errors that are common problems for basic/developmental writers. Each of these chapters is self-contained, so the instructor can feel free to vary the order of presentation of the chapters.

Both parts of the book may be used in a variety of settings, including formal classroom teaching, tutorial, and self-teaching. To assist the student in self-teaching, answers to roughly half of the book's exercises are included in a section at the back of this book (see Answers to Selected Exercises, pp. 251–256).

An Instructor's Edition of this text is also available, which includes the entire student text as well as an Instructor's Manual with suggestions for classroom use and a complete answer key to the exercises in Part II.

I want to thank the many individuals who contributed to the making of this book. Some helped indirectly through their views on writing and language acquisition. Foremost among those are Mina Shaughnessy, Mary Lawrence, William Strong, Janet Emig, Donald Murray, and Stephen Krashen. Among those who contributed directly are the following: Harry Hild, who was the first person I encountered to argue that written English was a kind of second language; Sandra Hunt, who introduced me to the concept of factor analysis; Karen Weidner, who helped type the manuscript; Karen Muskat, who helped proofread the manuscript; and all the Linguistics Department teaching assistants who used the material and made helpful suggestions.

I am also particularly indebted to Edward Mitchell-Hutchinson for his helpful suggestions throughout the process of developing the book and to Erica Appel for her help in the editing and production process.

Finally, I want to thank my students, who have taught me perhaps as much as I have taught them about the process of learning written English.

Audrey L. Reynolds

# TO THE STUDENT

Some of you have spoken English for as long as you can remember. Some of you may have learned to speak some other language, such as Spanish, Vietnamese, Farsi, Polish, Arabic, or Chinese, before you learned to speak English. But all of you have one thing in common: for all of you *written English* is a kind of *second language*—a slightly unfamiliar territory. You may even be so uncomfortable with written English that you try to avoid situations that force you to write.

This book is designed to make you more comfortable using written English by presenting it as a distinct variety of English—a variety with certain rules that differ from the rules we normally use when we speak. If you learn those rules, your writing will improve.

You are going to learn those rules first by reading about them and, second, by using them in your writing. You are already familiar with these two ways of learning. For example, if you have learned to play a musical instrument, you know that understanding everything your teacher says is not enough to make you proficient; you also have to learn how to *feel* what your teacher says. To use another example, if you have learned how to play a sport, you know you can understand what your coach says, but you also have to learn how to *feel* what he or she says. And you learn how to feel it by practicing.

You will be doing a lot of practicing in this course; specifically, you will be doing a great deal of writing. At this point, you may be feeling a little worried about making mistakes when you write. You may even be getting rather tense and anxious about the red marks that might appear on your papers after your teacher reads what you have written.

Let us pause briefly here to consider the subject of mistakes. We commonly make at least three different kinds of mistakes: good, embarrassing, and dangerous ones.

*Good mistakes* are the kind people have to make in order to learn how to do something new. For example, when you are learning to play a musical instrument, you make lots of mistakes as you develop a feel for the things your teacher has told you. Those mistakes are an important part of the learning process because you learn from them. Similarly, when you are learning to play a sport, you make many mistakes as you develop a *feel* for the things your coach has told you about, such things as how to spike a volleyball, guard an opponent in basketball, or tackle a player in football. Those errors are also a vital part of the learning process.

*Embarrassing mistakes* are the kind that make us feel foolish because we really do know better. They occur because we are careless. For example, it is embarrassing when you really have the ability to throw a baseball, but you aren't concentrating, and so you throw the ball ten feet over the first baseman's head. Such mistakes may make you angry with yourself, but the world won't come to an end because of them.

With dangerous mistakes, on the other hand, the consequences can be dire. If you drive a car at high speed on an icy highway, you are in serious danger. If you throw a lighted match into a gas tank, you should be prepared for trouble.

How do writing mistakes fit into this classification? Clearly, writing mistakes are not dangerous. Misspelling a word or forgetting to use a comma won't bring your world to an end. So that leaves us with the other two categories. How do writing mistakes fit into these categories? If you think about it for a moment, you will probably conclude that some writing mistakes are good mistakes, but others are embarrassing.

For an example of a good writing mistake, consider the kind of mistakes you will make when you are learning how to do something new in written English—the kind of mistake you will make as you try to develop a feel for a new rule of written English. This kind of mistake is an important step in the learning process. Therefore, instead of feeling upset about these errors, you should feel pleased with yourself because you are in the process of learning something new.

Embarrassing writing mistakes are those you make not from ignorance but from carelessness. Misspelling a word that you really do know how to spell is embarrassing. Because mistakes like these are easily corrected, we will consider them later.

So, for now, try not to worry about making mistakes, and just concentrate on learning each new idea as it is introduced. First, try to understand the idea, and then practice using it until you develop a feel for it. By the end of the course, you will know and understand the concept so well that it will come to you automatically when you write.

# CONTENTS

# PART II
## An Introduction to the Grammar of Written English 125

### Seven GRAMMAR AS A GAME 127

### Eight DEFINING THE SENTENCE: RECOGNIZING AND CORRECTING FRAGMENTS 137

### Nine DEFINING THE SENTENCE: RECOGNIZING AND CORRECTING RUN-ONS 155

## Ten PROOFREADING THE SENTENCE: PLURAL MARKERS AND SUBJECT-VERB AGREEMENT 172

## Eleven PROOFREADING THE SENTENCE: PAST TENSE AND PAST PARTICIPLE MARKERS 200

# EXPLORATIONS IN BASIC WRITING

# Part I

# AN INTRODUCTION TO THE PRINCIPLES OF GOOD WRITING

# ONE

# GETTING STARTED

## 1   THINKING ABOUT WRITING

All of us know how to talk. In fact, very few people can remember a time when they did not speak. Most of us have no difficulty holding conversations with our friends and relatives, but we don't feel as comfortable when we write. Why is this so?

To answer this question, we must consider how writing differs from speaking. Take a minute to write down all the differences you can think of between the two activities. Use the space provided below.

**Speaking:**

_____

_____

_____

_____

_____

_____

_____

**Writing:**

_____

_____

_____

_____

_____

_____

_____

As you can see from the lists you have made, writing and speaking differ in many ways. For one thing, written language has some unique features, like spelling and punctuation. Another difference is that in oral language the words vanish as soon as we have said them. Any grammar mistakes we make are likely to disappear before most of our listeners have had time to notice. In contrast, when we write, the words remain on the page for the readers to find and even study. Still other differences arise from the fact that when we speak, our listeners receive the message immediately. If they don't understand what we've said, they let us know right away. When we write, our words may not be read for hours, days, or even weeks. As a result, quite a bit of time may pass before we learn how well we communicated our ideas.

Because of all these differences between speaking and writing, we cannot simply write the way we talk. We have to learn how to use those features of the written language that will permit us to communicate effectively. In this book, you will learn about many of those features.

Before you begin to learn about the written language, it is important to discuss your feelings toward writing. If you like to write, you will enjoy working to improve your abilities. But if you dislike writing, you will not easily devote much time to it. Unfortunately, without a willingness to work, you will not improve as a writer. In order to help those of you who dislike writing, we will explore reasons for working to improve your writing.

Let's begin by asking whether you dislike writing. If the answer is yes, then ask yourself why you dislike it. If the answer is no, ask yourself why some people would dislike writing. Next, in the space below, list all the reasons you can think of.

_____

_____

_____

_____

_____

_____

_____

_____

In your list, you may have mentioned three of the reasons people often give. One reason some people give is their worry about making mistakes in spelling, punctuation, or grammar—mistakes the teacher will mark with a red pen. Their feelings are easy to understand, for none of us likes to have other people point out our mistakes, especially when the result may be a poor grade on a composition.

Other people dislike writing because they feel they have nothing to write about. When the teacher makes an assignment, they sit at their desks wondering what they are going to say in the composition. Those feelings are not unusual. Even professional writers sometimes find it difficult to express themselves in writing.

Still others dislike writing because it's a very lonely activity. When they talk, they are looking at people who may be smiling at them, asking questions, and encouraging them to express their ideas. But when they write, their only companions are a piece of paper and a pen, or just the keyboard and the screen on the computer. Being completely alone can be an unpleasant experience.

By now, you may have begun to wonder why people who dislike writing would ever want to work to improve. Next, then, we need to consider whether there are any reasons for liking it. If you do like to write, ask yourself why; if you do not, ask yourself why some people enjoy it. In the space below, list all the reasons you can think of.

_____

_____

_____

_____

_____

_____

_____

_____

_____

As you may have discovered, there are many reasons why some people like to write. Two are particularly useful for helping people understand why they might want to work to become better writers.

First, some people like having private time to daydream or think about their lives, their experiences, or their ideas and beliefs. They've learned that thinking "on paper"—that is, with a pen and paper or a computer keyboard to record their thoughts—leaves them with a written record of their thoughts that they can go back to later. Moreover, writing sometimes helps them to make their own thoughts clearer or even to discover new thoughts and new ideas that help them understand themselves or other people. Occasionally, those new thoughts and ideas can also make other people's lives richer and fuller.

The second reason is that it gives people an opportunity to keep a record of events in their lives. Having lived lives that are completely different from those of all other people, they have learned valuable things that perhaps no one else knows. By writing down their experiences as well as their thoughts about those experiences, they will be able to communicate what they've learned to others, including, possibly, their own children, grandchildren, or great-grandchildren.

Now that we've considered some of the reasons for liking writing, those of you who dislike it should be willing to consider the possibility that you might learn to like it better. If you're willing to consider that possibility, then you're ready to begin working to improve your writing.

## 2    THINKING ABOUT THE AUDIENCE: READERS VERSUS LISTENERS

In Section 1, you listed many differences between speaking and writing. In this section, we are going to concentrate on one of the differences: the fact that your audience is physically present when you talk but not when you write.

To understand the impact of the presence or absence of an audience, let's consider an example. Suppose you and a friend are shopping at a store, and you see a sofa that you think is really ugly. You can say, "Isn't *that* ugly!" and be sure that your friend will understand exactly what you mean. On the other hand, if you want to write to a friend and tell about the ugly sofa you saw, you will have to say more than "Isn't *that* ugly!" You will have to provide all kinds of details so that your friend will understand exactly what you are trying to communicate. We can sum up this point with a fundamental guideline for good writing:

> *Guideline 1:* Good writing must provide specific details, because the audience is not physically present.

The audience is not able to see what you see. As a result, when you write, you must give your reader all the information you can about what you see or, for that matter, about what you think.

Let's consider another example. Suppose you and a friend are talking, and you are telling your friend about an automobile accident you witnessed. You say: "I was walking down Lake Street, and I saw this terrible accident. This one guy had a cut on his forehead, and a woman was holding her neck and moaning." At this point, your friend interrupts to ask, "Exactly what happened?" So you explain that a man driving a BMW smashed into the back of a Toyota driven by a woman. The driver of the BMW hit the windshield and cut his forehead, and the woman suffered from a whiplash injury.

Because your friend was physically present when you were talking, he or she could interrupt you in order to ask for more information. When you write, however, your reader cannot interrupt. Therefore, you have to make sure that you provide all the information your reader will need in order to understand everything you want to communicate. Here, then, is a second fundamental guideline for good writing:

*Guideline 2:* Good writing gives the reader all necessary information; it doesn't make the reader guess what the writer is trying to say.

At this point, you may be wondering how you will know whether you've given the reader all necessary information. You don't want to give too little information because your reader will be confused. On the other hand, giving too many details will only bore your audience.

How do you know when you have written too little or too much? Unfortunately, there are no easy answers to this question. With experience, you will learn to answer this question for yourself through trial and error. For now, you can learn to look at your writing from the reader's standpoint—learn to approach your writing as if you were a reader who didn't know what was in the writer's mind.

To help you learn how to read your writing, we're going to use a technique called a *writing workshop exercise*. In this exercise, you will examine the work of other writers in order to help them discover how well they have communicated their ideas.

## Writing Workshop Exercise

➤ Read Composition 1 below in order to answer the following question: Where in the composition should the writer give more specific details so that the reader will have a better idea of what the writer's university is really like?

COMPOSITION 1: MY UNIVERSITY

I want to introduce you to Northeastern Illinois University. When you first arrive at Northeastern, you will notice many parking lots filled with cars. You will also notice several buildings.

At Northeastern, you will discover people everywhere. Some of the people are students, and some are professors. Others are staff members who work in the offices and the buildings of the university. But you can't always be sure who is a student and who is a professor or staff member.

The people do not all look alike, but they all have two things in common. They all live in the Chicago area, and they are all very busy.

Because there are so many busy people, you might think that Northeastern is a very noisy place, and you would be right. As you walk around the campus, you will hear lots of sounds.

As you might expect, with all these things to see and hear, Northeastern is a very interesting university.

Now read Composition 2 below in order to answer the following questions: Does the writer of this composition do a better job of describing the university than the writer of Composition 1 did? What is the difference between the two compositions?

COMPOSITION 2: MY UNIVERSITY

I want to introduce you to Northeastern Illinois University, which is located at the corner of Bryn Mawr and St. Louis, on the far northwest side of Chicago. When you first arrive at Northeastern, you will notice many parking lots filled with cars. You will also notice several buildings made of brick and glass. One building, which is called the Bee-hive, is six stories high. Three other buildings, the library, the science building, and the classroom building, are three or four stories high. One building, the Commuter Center, has two stories. The rest of the campus is like one long hallway that seems to go in all directions.

At Northeastern, you will discover people everywhere. Some of the people are students, and some are professors. Others are staff members who work in the offices and the buildings of the university. Most of the students are young and wear blue jeans and sweaters or shirts. Most of the professors and staff members are older and wear suits and ties if they are men, or they wear dresses or suits if they are women. But sometimes you will see a young professor in blue jeans and a sweater, or you will see an older student wearing a dress or a suit and tie, so you can't always be sure who is a student and who is a professor or staff member.

The people do not all look alike. Some are African-American, some are Asian-American, some are Hispanic-American, and some are White-American. But they all have two things in common. They all live in the Chicago area, and they are all very busy. Students are busy attending classes, studying, visiting the gameroom, having a cup of coffee, or talking with their friends. Professors are busy teaching their classes, working in their offices, having a cup of coffee, or talking with their friends. Staff members are busy working in their offices, having a cup of coffee, or talking with their friends.

Because there are so many busy people, you might think that Northeastern is a very noisy place, and you would be

right. As you walk around the campus, you will hear lots of
sounds. As you can guess, you will hear voices, but you will
also hear music. In the Commuter Center, music is always
playing. In the Unicorn, a lounge for students in the classroom building, you will often hear rock music coming from the
jukebox. In the A-wing, where the music department is located, you will hear students practicing on the piano or the
trumpet or the drums. In addition to music, sometimes you
will hear the sounds of movies in classrooms or the audito-
rium or the Unicorn.

As you might expect, with all these things to see and
hear, Northeastern is an interesting place to visit.

## 3   WRITING AS A PROCESS

Now that you've begun to think about the various ways speaking and writing
differ, you may be asking yourself how anybody ever succeeds at writing—first, at
finding ideas to write about, then at providing all the information the reader needs
to understand the ideas, while also presenting the ideas in good sentences with no
grammatical errors, no misspelled words, and no punctuation problems. How can
anybody do all those things at the very same time?

The answer is a simple one: Almost no writer succeeds in this effort, and
fortunately, no writer has to because of an advantage that writing has over speaking.
Let's consider that advantage.

When you're speaking, your audience is physically present as you try to
express your ideas. As a result, you sometimes discover that you have used a word
or phrase that you really wish you hadn't because it doesn't quite say what you
really mean or perhaps because it has made your listener upset or angry. When that
happens, the best thing to do is to say, "That isn't what I meant. Let me try again."
But, in a sense, the damage is done; the word or phrase has affected the listener.

When you're writing, the audience is not physically present, so you don't
have to be as worried about using a wrong word or phrase when you try to express
your ideas. Later, when you have had a chance to read what you have written, you
can erase or scratch out any word or phrase you want to change before the reader
sees it. As a result, when writing, you have more freedom to experiment with words
and sentences as you work to express your ideas. So you don't have to get the words
and sentences right the first time. You have a chance to keep improving them until
you get them right.

The chance to keep improving a piece of written communication is what some people call the *writing process*. Experienced writers are familiar with that process. They know that a finished piece of writing does not occur automatically. Instead, it grows and develops through several stages as the writer seeks to communicate his or her ideas clearly and effectively. This point brings us to our third guideline for good writing:

> **Guideline 3:** A finished piece of writing goes through a process of several stages as it develops, including prewriting, drafting, and proofreading.

As you become more experienced as a writer, you will learn more about the stages in the writing process. In this chapter, we will discuss three of those stages: *prewriting*, *drafting*, and *proofreading*.

What is prewriting? The prefix *pre-* tells us that the word means "before writing." Prewriting is everything that writers do as they get ready to write the sentences and paragraphs of an essay or composition. It might take place inside the writer's head, but usually the most productive prewriting is done on paper with a pen or pencil, or a typewriter or word processor.

How do writers get ready to write? The answer to that question is ultimately very complicated, because there are many prewriting techniques. In this section, we'll consider one prewriting technique called *brainstorming* (a word that means, "letting your brain run wild as if there's a storm in your head"). When we brainstorm, we write down every idea that comes into our heads. For instance, suppose you are asked to write a composition describing the neighborhood where you live. To prepare yourself for writing, you can make a list of every idea that occurs to you as you think about the subject.

When you've completed the prewriting stage, you're ready for the second stage in the writing process: *drafting*. In this stage, writers develop the material they have already collected into sentences and paragraphs, but they don't worry much about misspelled words, missing commas, or grammatical errors. Instead, they concentrate on getting their ideas written down on paper, knowing that they'll have time to make corrections later.

After the draft has been completed, a number of things may happen, and we'll consider those later. For now, we'll mention just one of these things: *proofreading*— the stage in the writing process when writers check their sentences to eliminate mistakes. We'll discuss proofreading in more detail later in this chapter.

Now that we've considered the first two stages in the writing process, you're ready to become comfortable using them. In order to help you learn to be more relaxed about making mistakes when you prewrite and draft, in this chapter and in later chapters you will get an opportunity to write what we call *journal assignments*. In journal assignments, you are supposed to worry about the ideas you want to communicate in your writing and not about mistakes. Through these assignments, you will learn how much easier it is to get your ideas down on paper when you aren't worrying about spelling and grammar.

Then you'll be ready to write what we will call *composition assignments*. In these assignments, you will not only prewrite and draft your ideas but also proofread your writing in order to create a more formal product for your reader.

## Journal Assignment

➤ Imagine that a local newspaper has asked you to write an article about the neighborhood where you live or about the campus of your school. Prepare yourself for writing by brainstorming about all the things you can see, hear, and smell. Then write a description of either your neighborhood or your school. Be sure to give your readers lots of specific details and to tell them everything they will need to know in order to fully understand what your neighborhood or school is like.

## 4   FINDING DETAILS TO USE IN WRITING

In Section 3, you read about one way to find details to use in your writing—brainstorming. In this section, we will consider some other ways of finding details.

One way is to observe the world closely. Much of the time we take the world around us for granted. We're so busy working, studying, or socializing that we don't really see the people, objects, or activities in our world. Good writers have learned that the things we take for granted can be very interesting if we spend time observing them carefully. For instance, the palms of our hands are remarkably complicated instruments with lines that go in a number of directions, lines of varying lengths, lines that make a variety of patterns. A desk in a classroom is also remarkable. It has its own peculiar shape that makes it different from desks in homes or offices, and drawings or graffiti may have been etched on it that reveal things about the people who've used it in the past. By closely observing objects and people in the world around them, writers find concrete details that will help the reader understand the writer's world.

To see how this technique works, take a few minutes to look carefully at the room around you. Then in the space provided below, write down as many details as you can.

_____

_____

_____

_____

_____

_____

_____

_____

_____

_____

_____

_____

_____

_____

_____

Another way of finding details is to use your brain to re-create the world inside your head. All of us occasionally use our imaginations to daydream about the way we wish the world could be—about people we wish would ask us for dates, about jobs we wish we could get, about homes we would like to have. Writers use those daydreams as sources of details. They visualize scenes in their minds and then describe those scenes in detail for the reader. Writers use the same technique to write about their memories. They re-create the original situation inside their heads in order to find the details they need.

To help you become more skilled at re-creating the world, we're going to do a couple of prewriting exercises that writers sometimes use to find ideas and concrete details. The first technique is called *free writing*. When writers *free write*, they relax and write down everything that comes into their minds, without scratching out a single word. In Figure 1.1 on the next page you can see what happened when one writer did free writing on the topic "My Favorite Spot."

Another prewriting technique that experienced writers sometimes use is called *free-association clustering*. When writers use this technique, they begin with a topic they are thinking about using in a piece of writing. They put that topic in the middle of a blank piece of paper and draw a circle around it. Then they relax to see

My favorite spot. Where's my favorite spot? Maybe the beach. I love it, but always too many people. Too many people drive me nuts. I think I'd rather — I think my favorite spot is actually at home. Of all places. In my room — All of my favorite things — stereo, cassettes, CD's. I put on headphones and listen to music as loud as I want. I let the music carry me away. I pretend I'm on TV, singing and dancing with Lisa. I imagine being able to dance like Michael Jackson. Other things in my room: Michael Jordan poster, pennants from the Bulls championship years, autographed program. Walter Payton poster. Bears pennant from the year they won the Super Bowl. That was an exciting year. What else? My Ryne Sandberg poster, but I don't think the Cubs will ever win the pennant. What else? My catcher's mitt. Dad gave that to me on my birthday, fifteenth birthday. I played catcher three years and used that mitt for every game. I put that mitt on — I feel like Carlton Fisk. Or Roy Campanella, my dad's hero. I feel like I could be in the majors. What other details? I wrote about my music and sports stuff. There's furniture too, a bed, a desk, a dresser. Also a bookcase with my schoolbooks. And a bulletin board over the desk with a lot of snapshots from over the years.

**Figure 1.1**   An example of freewriting.

what will be the first thing they think of. When that first thought comes, they make an arrow from the circle before writing the first thought. Then they write down all the thoughts they have about that "first thought." The writer in Figure 1.2 on the next page, for example, was thinking about her kitchen. The first thought that came to her was "a cheerful room." When she thought about why the room was cheerful, she wrote down the words "yellow walls," "yellow place mats on the table," "sunlight streaming in through big windows." After she had written all her thoughts on cheerfulness, she then returned to the topic of her kitchen for another association. This time she thought of the word "bright," which then triggered another set of associations, and so on. She kept going until she had a whole page filled with associations.

So, to find details, you can observe the world around you directly, or you can use techniques like free writing and free-association clustering to help you re-create in words the world you see inside your head.

## COMPOSITION ASSIGNMENT

Each of us has certain places that we like or dislike more than other places on earth. Choose a place that you consider one of your "favorite spots" or choose a place that you dislike intensely. Then write a composition in which you describe that location. Try to convince your reader that the place you've chosen is worth visiting or is better to avoid. Before you write a draft of the composition, spend quite a bit of time prewriting. Use free writing, free-association clustering, and brainstorming to find concrete details you can use to help your reader understand why you feel the way you do about your chosen place.

## 5   SENTENCE COMBINING IN WRITTEN ENGLISH: RELATIVE PRONOUNS

In Section 1, we thought about many ways in which writing and speaking differ. Then in Sections 2 and 3, we focused on two ways in which they differ—ways relating to the presence or absence of the audience. Now we're going to consider a third difference that involves the language we use. When we speak, we produce sounds that travel through the air and disappear immediately after we say them. When we write, we produce marks on paper that will stay on the page for as long as we want them to.

Why is this difference important? To answer this question, we need to con-

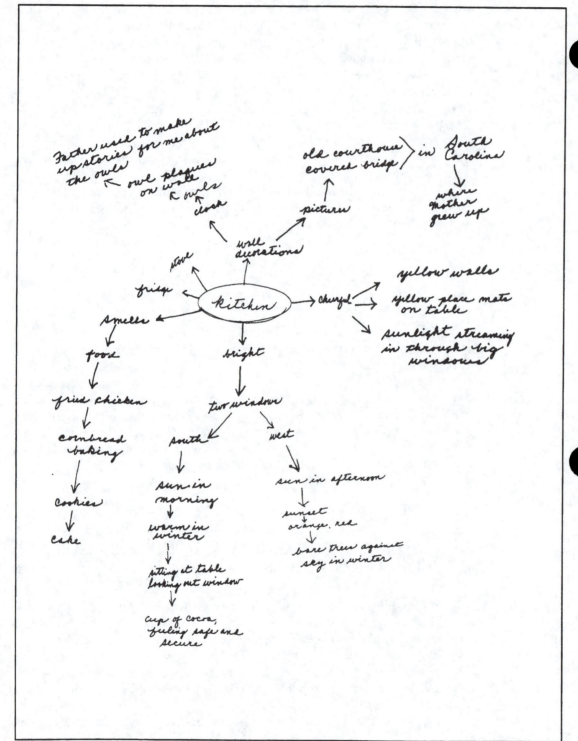

**Figure 1.2**   Free-association clustering.

sider how listeners are affected by the fact that speech is made up of sounds that disappear rapidly. When we speak, our listeners only get a little bit of time to understand our message before it vanishes completely. But listeners usually succeed in understanding our ideas, even though time places them under a great deal of pressure. They succeed because we speakers help them, even though we may not realize it. When we speak, we often produce many short, simple sentences, as the following passage illustrates:

```
I really dislike Greta. She's just impossible. She's always
telling lies. Her whole life is a lie. She drives me nuts. Ev-
erything she does is based on secrets. Her appearance is a
lie. She has blonde hair. She dyes it. She wants to hide the
gray. She can't see very well. She doesn't want anyone to
know. She can't wear contact lenses. There's something about
her eyes. I think she has astigmatism. Anyway, she can't wear
contacts, but she won't wear glasses. She ends up walking
around half blind.
```

A passage like this doesn't bother listeners. They're so busy working to understand the message before the sounds disappear that they don't notice how much the speaker repeats herself as she communicates her ideas.

For readers, however, this passage is quite irritating. They are bothered by the repetition, which they notice because the message doesn't disappear. They would be happier with a passage like the following one, which is made up of longer, more complicated sentences:

```
I really dislike Greta because her whole life is based on
lies and secrets. Her appearance is deceptive. She has blonde
hair, which she dyes, because she wants to hide the gray. She
doesn't want people to know that she can't see very well, so
she refuses to wear glasses. She says that she would wear
contact lenses, but she can't because she has astigmatism. So
she walks around half blind.
```

Readers prefer such sentences for at least two reasons. First, they want the writer to produce sentences that communicate ideas effectively without unnecessary repetition. The second reason has to do with what we can think of as the *rhythm* of language. Notice how the first passage about Greta seems choppy: sentences start, then stop, then start, then stop. The meaning is clear, but the sentences in the second passage *flow* much more freely, and this makes readers comfortable. If the writer must produce longer, more complicated sentences in order to accomplish these goals, readers don't mind because they can have as much time as they need to understand the message, which won't disappear.

As you might expect, writers who want to produce such sentences will need to spend more time working on sentences than speakers do. Fortunately, writers can get that extra time by taking advantage of the fact that writing is a process. After they've drafted a piece of writing, they can go back to examine their sentences in order to make sure they've discovered the most effective way of communicating their ideas before they allow the reader to see the finished product.

If you're going to become more comfortable producing the kind of writing readers like to read, you will need to practice working on sentences to find the most effective way of communicating particular ideas. In each chapter in the first part of the book, you will get an opportunity to get that kind of practice through a method called *sentence combining*.

Let's begin by considering the two passages we discussed earlier in this section. Obviously, most of the sentences in the second passage are longer than those in the first. Also, those longer sentences are combinations of sentences from the first passage. If you look carefully at the sentences in the second passage, you will notice that several connecting words were used to combine the sentences, connecting words you use when you speak—words like *and, but, so,* and *that.* As you can guess, one way to combine sentences is to use an appropriate connecting word.

In this section, we will focus on three of the connectors that are commonly used in the written language to produce longer, more complicated sentences—the words *that, who,* and *which.*

Consider the following pairs of sentences:

Bob met a woman. She likes football.
Elaine has a brother. He collects stamps.
José bought a car. It was five years old.
David has a coat. It is falling apart.

Using what you know about spoken English, you can combine each of these pairs of sentences into one sentence in at least two ways:

Bob met a woman that likes football.
Bob met a woman who likes football.

Elaine has a brother that collects stamps.
Elaine has a brother who collects stamps.

José bought a car that was five years old.
José bought a car which was five years old.

David has a coat that is falling apart.
David has a coat which is falling apart.

The words *that, who,* and *which* in these sentences are examples of what we're going to call *sentence connectors*—words that can be used to combine two sentences into one longer sentence. The sentence connectors *that, who,* and *which* can be used to combine two sentences if each of the sentences has a word (or group of words) that refers to the same thing. For example, in the sentences

**Bob met a woman. She likes football.**

*a woman* and *she* refer to the same person, so the sentences can be combined to say:

**Bob met a woman who likes football.**

Similarly, in the sentences

**José bought a car. It was five years old.**

*a car* and *it* refer to the same thing, so the sentences can be combined as:

**José bought a car that was five years old.**

As you learn more about written English, you will discover that the rules for using these words—which are known as *relative pronouns*—are rather complex. However, at this point in your development as a writer, you should remember two things when you are using relative pronouns to combine sentences.

First, make sure that you use the correct relative pronoun. If you examine the sentences that we considered earlier in this section, you will discover that the relative pronoun *that* can be used to combine all the pairs of sentences, but the relative pronouns *who* and *which* are used in only some of the sentences. What makes the difference? The relative pronoun *who* can be used only after words that refer to *people* (for example, *a brother* or *a woman*). The relative pronoun *which* can be used only after words that refer to *things* or *animals* (for example, *a car* or *a lion*). But the relative pronoun *that* can be used for *people, things,* and *animals.*

Second, remember that you can combine the two sentences with a relative pronoun when each of the sentences contains a word (or group of words) that refers to the same thing. The relative pronoun that you use should come immediately after that word in the first sentence. For example, consider the following pairs of sentences:

Susan bought the book. Her father wanted it.
The stereo system cost $2,500. My uncle bought it.

Since each of these pairs contains words that refer to the same thing, they can be combined using relative pronouns:

Susan bought the book that her father wanted.
Susan bought the book which her father wanted.

The stereo system that my uncle bought cost $2,500.
The stereo system which my uncle bought cost $2,500.

Notice that the relative pronoun is placed after the word in the first sentence that refers to the thing, no matter where that word occurs in the sentence.

Now that you have some understanding of how sentence-combining exercises work, you're ready to try an exercise on your own.

## Sentence-Combining Practice

➤ Combine the following pairs of sentences using relative pronouns. There may be more than one possible way of combining them.

1. I met a girl. She lives on the fourth floor of my building.

_____

_____

2. The woman is the mother of four. She is a doctor.

_____

_____

3. The men play poker once a week. They live down the block.

_____

_____

4. A music teacher will sing at my wedding. She is my sister's best friend.

_____

_____

5. Jennifer hates rude people. They cut into the line at movies.

_____

_____

6. Pedro has a history professor. She has a great sense of humor.

_____

_____

7. Bob and Mark were searching for the necklace. My little sister had hidden it.

_____

_____

8. The car should be towed away. It hasn't been moved in three months.

_____

_____

9. The biology professor talks too fast. He has a bald head and a beard.

_____

_____

10. The movie was very interesting. My aunt recommended it.

_____

_____

11. My Lai found a new apartment. It has a view of the river.

_____

_____

12. The snow caused the garage roof to collapse. It fell last night.

_____

_____

## Sentence-Creating Practice

➤ Write ten sentences of your own in which you use the sentence connectors *that, who,* or *which.*

1. _____

_____

2. _____

_____

3. _____

_____

4. _____

_____

5. _____

_____

6. _____

_____

7. _____

_____

8. _____

_____

9. _____

_____

10. _____

_____

## 6 SENTENCE COMBINING: PUTTING IT TOGETHER

In this section, you're going to have an opportunity to use what you have learned in this chapter and what you already know about sentence combining.

➤ On your own paper, take each group of sentences and combine them into one sentence. For some groups, you may wish to use one of the relative pronouns *who, which,* or *that*. For others, you may want to use connecting words that you already know, words such as *and, but,* or *so.*

### MY FAVORITE SPOT

1. Everyone has one special place.
2. They really like that place.

3. My favorite spot is a campground.
4. It is in Wisconsin.
5. It is on the shores of Lake Michigan.

6. The campground has lots of campsites.
7. They are not close together.
8. My friends and I don't feel surrounded by people.

9. We put up our tent.
10. We build our fire.
11. We pretend that we are all alone in the wilderness.

12. At night we go walking on the beach.
13. We look out on Lake Michigan.
14. It stretches all the way to the horizon.

15. We see only the water.
16. The water is dark blue with little patches of white.
17. The waves make the patches.

18. We look up at the sky.
19. The sky is dark blue.
20. We can see the stars.
21. They seem close enough to touch.

22. We return to our campsite.
23. It is close to the lake.
24. We hear the waves.
25. The waves rush against the shore.
26. They lull us to sleep.

## 7   THINKING ABOUT PROOFREADING

Before you turn in your composition on your favorite or least favorite spot, we must consider one other major difference between speaking and writing. When you speak, no teacher marks your errors with a red pen; however, when you write, teachers do mark your mistakes.

To avoid making mistakes, you can become familiar with the rules for written English, which you will be learning in the second part of the book. You can also become skilled at proofreading, the last stage in the writing process. After you have written down all your ideas, you should read over the composition and correct any mistakes you find. Why do you need to proofread? As we discussed in Section 3, it's easier to concentrate first on getting your ideas down clearly. You can look for mistakes in grammar and punctuation later.

To become a skilled proofreader, you need to practice—and you will get many chances to practice proofreading as you work through the exercises in Part II of this book. You should also begin to proofread each composition assignment. At first, you may not be sure what mistakes to look for, but as you learn more about written English, you will learn more about the common mistakes you make. With experience you will become better and better at proofreading.

For now, you can practice using a couple of tips that professional proofreaders use. (1) Proofread "backwards." Start at the end of the essay, proofreading the last sentence. Then proofread backwards, one sentence at a time from the end of the essay to the beginning. As strange as it may seem, proofreading in this way makes it easier to find mistakes because you cannot be distracted by the ideas in the essay when you're reading backwards. (2) Use a ruler or a blank piece of paper to cover everything in the essay except the sentence you're proofreading at the moment. In that way you can focus all your attention on finding the mistakes in that sentence.

## Proofreading Practice

➤ Proofread the composition that you wrote in Section 4 for mistakes in grammar, spelling, and punctuation.

# TWO

# ORGANIZING YOUR IDEAS

## 1 FINDING TOPICS FOR WRITING

In Chapter 1, we talked about a few things that make writing a harder, sometimes more unpleasant activity than speaking. We also talked about one aspect of writing that makes it more pleasant—the fact that you get the chance to keep improving your words and sentences before you show them to the audience. In this chapter, we will explore more of the differences between speaking and writing that can make writing a more enjoyable activity. In this section, we're going to discuss one of those advantages. As we do so, we'll be considering the question of how you can discover subjects to write about.

Let's begin by discussing a situation that all of us have experienced—the moment when someone makes you really angry, but for various reasons you don't respond the way you would like to. Perhaps you're angry with a family member, a friend, or someone you're dating, and you are so upset that you say all the wrong things. Or perhaps you are angry with a boss, a teacher, or a police officer, but you feel compelled to keep your mouth shut in order to avoid getting into serious trouble.

Later, when you're in your bedroom or your bathroom, you may look at the mirror and imagine that you're telling that person what you wish you had said. As you're doing so, you may get very frustrated. You're thinking of all these wonderful things you could have said, but no one will ever hear them.

Writers do not experience this frustration because they can capture those terrific ideas on paper and use them later in a piece of writing. When writers record such ideas, they often produce some of their best writing because they really care about communicating the ideas they're developing in the essay. They aren't writing just because they have to. Here we find our fourth guideline for good writing:

> *Guideline 4:* Writers produce their best writing when they care about the ideas they're presenting.

To see this principle in practice, let's examine two compositions that were written by the same writer.

## Writing Workshop Exercise

➤ As you read the following compositions, keep these questions in mind: (1) Which essay do you think the writer wrote because he or she had to write something? (2) Which essay do you think the writer wanted to write?

### COMPOSITION 1: HOW TO DO THE LAUNDRY

Sooner or later, almost everyone has to do the laundry, but many people do not really know <u>how</u> to do the laundry. In case you are one of those people, here are some simple tips that will make the task easier when you visit the Laundromat.

First of all, sort the dirty clothes and linens into several piles, depending on the colors of the fabrics and the laundry instructions on the labels that indicate what water temperature should be used. After the laundry is sorted into piles, take one pile and put it in a washing machine. Then add the detergent, set the dial for the right temperature, and put your money in the slot. When one machine is operating, take the second pile of clothes and follow the same procedure until all the clothes are in washers.

When the clothes are washed, remove them from the machines and put them in the dryers. Be sure to check the fabric labels so that you set the dial at the right temperature. Also, add a sheet of fabric softener so that your clothes

will smell fresh and be static-free. When the dryer is ready,
insert your coins in the slot.

    After the clothes and linens are dry, you should fold
the linens carefully, and put the clothing on hangers to
avoid wrinkles.


COMPOSITION 2: HOW TO BE A TERRIBLE GUEST

    All of us occasionally get invited to parties where
there will be lots of strangers. If you want to make sure that
your host and hostess will invite you to other parties that
they give, here are some hints that you can use.

    As you're getting ready for the party, you should think
carefully about what you're going to wear. If you think most
of the people at the party will be wearing jeans, you should
really dress up. If you're a man, you should wear a suit and a
tie. If you're a woman, you should wear a fancy party dress.
But if you think that most of the people will be dressed up,
then you should wear your oldest pair of dirty jeans and a
T-shirt.

    When you have decided what you're going to wear, you
should plan to get dressed quickly because you want to make
sure that you get to the party before it's supposed to begin.
You want to see the looks on your host and hostess's faces
when you arrive much too early.

    When your host asks you what you want to drink, you
should tell him that you would like freshly squeezed orange
juice, fresh pineapple juice, or expensive champagne. When
your host tells you that he is sorry that he doesn't have any,
you should sigh and agree to drink whatever he has.

    When you're introduced to the first guests who arrive,

you should tell them about all the problems you're having with your sister. You should keep talking until the strangers excuse themselves in order to go to the washroom or go to the kitchen to get something to eat or drink. After the other guests arrive, you should pick up a book or magazine and begin to read it because you want people to know that you're very intelligent.

Before you leave the party, you should walk through the room bumping into people so that they will know that you are there. If you bump them hard enough, they will spill their drinks, and you can be sure that they will have noticed you. Then you should tell the hostess that you have to leave early because you have another party to attend. That way, she will know how lucky she is to know such a popular person.

Then you can go home knowing that your host and hostess will be sure to ask you to their next party.

## Journal Assignment

➤ Write a list of all the things you can think of that you dislike intensely. In your list you might include chores that you do around the house, people who really get on your nerves, opinions that you find very offensive, sports or activities you hate, and so on. Then make a list of all the things you can think of that you like very much, such as chores you enjoy, people you find delightful, sports or activities you enjoy, and opinions you believe in strongly. In this way, you're developing a list of possible topics that you care deeply about. You can add to this list throughout the course and use it to help you find writing topics for later assignments.

## 2    THINKING ABOUT ORGANIZATION

In this section, we're going to consider another advantage that writing has over speaking—the fact that you have an opportunity to plan and organize your message.

When you talk to your friends, the conversation just happens. You cannot plan what you are going to say very far in advance because your listener may interrupt at any minute and ask a question or make a comment that forces you to change your plan. Sometimes the questions and comments help to clarify your opinions, but at other times they force you to talk about things you really don't want to talk about. In contrast, when you write, in the absence of a listener who can interrupt you, you are free to speak your mind.

Once you know you have the freedom to say what you really want to say, then you can plan what you're going to say in advance. That is, you have a chance to *organize* your ideas in order to present them clearly. What is more, you are expected to organize them so that you will make it easier for the reader to follow your ideas. This brings us to our fifth guideline for good writing:

> *Guideline 5:* In good writing, the ideas are presented in an orga-
> nized, orderly manner.

Now you need to become comfortable using various ways of organizing your ideas. In this chapter, we're going to concentrate on one possible way of organizing your ideas—*chronological order*—which, simply put, is the order in which events happen in time. Most stories as well as history books are organized in this way. Whatever occurred first is told first, what happened second is described second, and so on to the end.

## Journal Assignment

➤ Write a description in chronological order of what you think would be the perfect way to spend a Saturday night. Imagine that someone has promised to give you as much money as you need to pay for the evening's activities. First, brainstorm to think of the things you might like to do. Then plan your evening carefully, choosing the activities you would most like to do. Then use brainstorming, freewriting, or free-association clustering to find concrete details to use in describing the activities. As you write, be sure to put all the details in chronological order.

## 3   MORE ON THE WRITING PROCESS

In Chapter 1, we looked at three stages in the writing process: prewriting, drafting, and proofreading. In this section, we're going to examine where planning fits into this process.

As you might expect, writers often organize their ideas during the prewriting stage. They brainstorm for details and then arrange those details in order, using an outline or similar tool as a blueprint for the essay.

Sometimes, however, after the prewriting stage, when the writer is drafting the composition, an interesting thing happens. Suddenly the writer has a brand new idea that he or she wants to include in the essay, but the idea belongs much earlier in the essay. Can the writer include that idea and still produce an organized piece of writing? Writers can do so if they're aware that there are more stages in the writing process than the three we discussed in Chapter 1. In this section, we will focus on two of these: scanning and revising.

*Scanning* is what writers do when they need a break from drafting. They may need a break because their fingers are getting "writer's cramp" or "typist's cramp," or their brains may have run out of ideas to write about. During the break, writers go back to the beginning of the piece and *scan* it; that is, they *read* it rapidly to see how well they like it.

When they find something they don't like—they may dislike a word or a sentence or even a whole paragraph—they may decide it's time for *revising*. Revising is what writers do when they discover, in the middle of a piece, that they want to improve it by making some changes in earlier parts. To do so, they will have to rewrite the whole composition. When writers realize that revision is necessary, they may either start rewriting immediately, or they may just keep drafting, making notes to use later during the rewriting stage. For instance, the writer might write in the margin, "Add this idea at the end of the second paragraph," or "Find a better word." Or the writer might scratch out a word or a sentence or a whole paragraph, before writing a better version.

Writers who scan and then revise do, of course, produce pages that look messy. Writing can indeed be a very messy process while it's occurring. But you should keep in mind that the writer is the only person who sees the untidy pages. Before showing it to someone else, the writer will rewrite the piece to create a neat, clean copy of the finished product.

In Figure 2.1 on the next page you can examine a page from the first draft of a section in this book that you've already read: the section called "To the Student." Look at the figure and then turn to page ix to see what the section looked like when it was finished.

## 4   THINKING ABOUT PARAGRAPHS

Now we are going to discuss yet another major difference between speaking and writing. When you speak, of course you don't speak in paragraphs, and so you never have to think in terms of where one paragraph ends and another begins. However, when you write, you do have to decide when to begin a new paragraph, and, as you might expect, it is not always easy to make this decision.

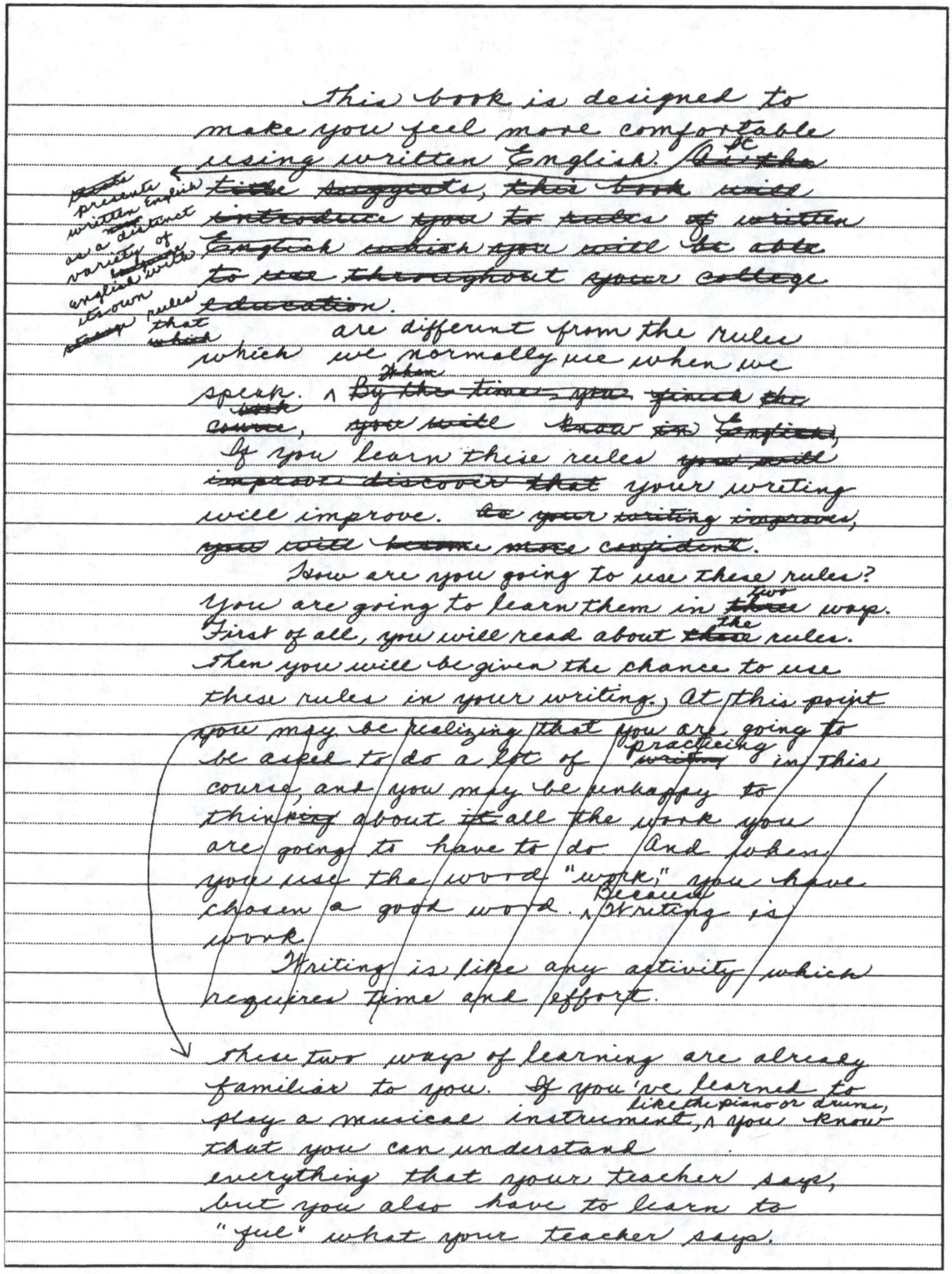

This book is designed to make you feel more comfortable using written English. It ~~As the title suggests, this book will introduce you to rules of written English which you will be able to use throughout your college education.~~ presents written English as a distinct variety of English with its own rules that are different from the rules which we normally use when we speak. ~~By the time you finish the course, you will know in English,~~ If you learn these rules ~~you will improve discover that~~ your writing will improve. ~~As your writing improves, you will become more confident.~~

How are you going to use these rules? You are going to learn them in ~~three~~ two ways. First of all, you will read about ~~these~~ the rules. Then you will be given the chance to use these rules in your writing. ~~At this point you may be realizing that you are going to be asked to do a lot of ~~writing~~ practicing in this course, and you may be unhappy to thinking about it all the work you are going to have to do. And when you use the word "work," you have chosen a good word. Because Writing is work.~~

~~Writing is like any activity which requires time and effort.~~

These two ways of learning are already familiar to you. If you've learned to play a musical instrument, like the piano or drums, you know that you can understand everything that your teacher says, but you also have to learn to "feel" what your teacher says.

Figure 2.1 A first draft.

Let's begin by defining the word *paragraph*. A paragraph is *a section of a composition that deals with a particular point.* This definition indicates, then, that a new paragraph should begin when a writer moves from one point in the composition to another. But you may be wondering how a writer knows when he or she has reached a new point. This question may be especially puzzling to those of you who've noticed that a newspaper writer may take several paragraphs to make a particular point, and many of the paragraphs are only one sentence long. Should you, therefore, assume that a writer starts a new paragraph every time he or she starts a new sentence?

The answer to this question is that it depends on what kind of writing you're doing. This answer may seem less strange if we briefly consider one of the similarities between writing and speaking. Just as you're expected to speak in different ways to your friends, family, teachers, or total strangers, so when you write, you're expected to write differently in different situations.

Therefore, if you're writing for a newspaper, you may be expected to write short paragraphs, many of which are only one sentence long. If you're writing an essay or a composition in an academic setting, then you will usually be expected to write much longer paragraphs.

So how can you tell when to start a new paragraph? Even experienced writers at times find it hard to explain why they decided to begin a new paragraph, but at other times their decision is easily explained. In this book, we're going to concentrate on paragraphing decisions that are easy to explain so that you can begin to develop an understanding of how paragraphs work.

For the moment, we will look at paragraphs in a way that can be especially useful when you're using chronological order to organize your ideas.

Let us begin by talking about bees. These insects have more to do with paragraphs than you might think. If you have ever studied bees, you may know that beehives sometimes have a problem with overpopulation. When a beehive reaches the point where there are too many inhabitants in the hive, the bees divide the population into two groups: those who stay in the hive and those who leave to form another hive someplace else. The same thing can happen when an author writes. The ideas in the sentences develop and grow until a paragraph gets too long. When that happens, the author breaks the idea into two or three or more paragraphs.

So experienced writers sometimes use length as a way of deciding when to begin new paragraphs. They instinctively know when paragraphs have become too long, and in time you too will come to know. You can begin to develop that knowledge by analyzing pieces of writing from the point of view of why the writers paragraphed them in particular ways.

You can start by examining the two compositions in Section 1 of this chapter. The first thing you'll notice is that "How to Do the Laundry" is much shorter than "How to Be a Terrible Guest." Not surprisingly, the shorter composition is divided into only four paragraphs, while the longer is divided into seven.

As you look more closely at the two essays, you will discover that the first writer had a small number of details and so needed only a few paragraphs: one paragraph introducing the topic of the essay, one explaining how to wash clothes, one describing how to use a dryer, and one concluding paragraph telling the reader what to do when the clothes are dry. In contrast, the writer of the other essay had many more details and so decided to break it up into several paragraphs: one paragraph introducing the topic, one explaining how to dress for the party, four paragraphs giving specific tips on how to behave at the party, and one concluding paragraph telling the reader what will happen after the party.

After examining those essays, you should feel that you have a better understanding of how writers use length as a way of deciding when to start a new paragraph. Throughout Part I, you will continue to develop your awareness of paragraphs so that in time you will behave like an experienced writer: you will "just know" when to start a new paragraph.

## COMPOSITION ASSIGNMENT

As part of this chapter, you've examined a composition titled "How to Be a Terrible Guest." Think of some topic that you would like to develop into a composition called "How to Be a Terrible _____," where you will fill in the blank. The list of possible topics you began in Section 1 of this chapter may help you get started. If not, here are some possible topics that you might consider using:

| | | |
|---|---|---|
| car driver | bus driver | cab driver |
| boss | date | supermarket checker |
| friend | waiter | salesclerk |

Once you have a topic, prewrite to find concrete details. Then organize your ideas using chronological order. As you're writing the composition, use what you've learned about paragraphing and about the writing process—drafting, scanning, revising, and proofreading.

## 5   SENTENCE COMBINING IN WRITTEN ENGLISH: CHRONOLOGICAL ORDER

In Chapter 1, you learned how to use sentence connectors to combine two sentences into one longer sentence. In this chapter, we're going to concentrate on sentence connectors that you can use when you wish to express chronological relationships between sentences.

One common time relationship you can write about concerns one event followed by another event:

Mark washed the car. Then he cooked dinner.

There are several ways to combine these two sentences:

Mark washed the car before he cooked dinner.
Mark cooked dinner after he washed the car.
Before Mark cooked dinner, he washed the car.
After Mark washed the car, he cooked dinner.
Mark washed the car; subsequently, he cooked dinner.
Mark washed the car; afterwards, he cooked dinner.

All these sentences mean exactly the same thing. The sentence connectors *before, after, subsequently,* and *afterwards* can all be used to describe one event followed by another event, but you will notice that the words are used in different ways. For one thing, the words *before* and *after* appear in two places: at the beginning or in the middle of a sentence. *Subsequently* and *afterwards* only appear in the middle. The punctuation rules for the connectors are also different. When the words *before* and *after* come at the beginning of a sentence, a comma is inserted before the second part of the sentence, but when the words come between the two parts of the sentence, no punctuation mark is required. On the other hand, when the words *subsequently* and *afterwards* are used as connectors, a *semicolon* (;) goes before the word and a comma after it.

To help you remember the differences between the two kinds of connectors, we're going to call words like *before* and *after*, which can appear in two places, *two-place connectors.* We will call words like *subsequently* and *afterwards,* which use semicolons, *semicolon connectors.*

Now let's consider another common chronological relationship—one that concerns two events that happen at almost the same time. Consider the following sentences:

Philip entered the room. Right away, he saw Mary.
Anna reached the corner. Right away, she saw a fire truck.

These sentences can be combined by putting the two-place connectors *when* or *as* at the beginning of the event that comes first, as in the following sentences:

When Philip entered the room, he saw Mary.
Philip saw Mary when he entered the room.
When Anna reached the corner, she saw a fire truck.
Anna saw a fire truck when she reached the corner.

As Philip entered the room, he saw Mary.
Philip saw Mary as he entered the room.
As Anna reached the corner, she saw a fire truck.
Anna saw a fire truck as she reached the corner.

Another common time relationship concerns two events that happened at exactly the same time and both continued for a period of time.

Bill was watching television. At the same time, Jane took a nap.
Irma was cooking dinner. At the same time, Mario read the news-
    paper.

Because the events in these sentences go on for a period of time (they are not over in a second), sentences like these can be combined using the two-place connector *while*:

While Bill was watching television, Jane took a nap.
Jane took a nap while Bill was watching television.
Bill was watching television while Jane took a nap.
While Jane took a nap, Bill was watching television.

While Irma was cooking dinner, Mario read the newspaper.
Mario read the newspaper while Irma was cooking dinner.
While Mario read the newspaper, Irma was cooking dinner.
Irma was cooking dinner while Mario read the newspaper.

These sentences might also be combined by using the semicolon connector *in the meantime:*

Bill was watching television; in the meantime, Jane took a nap.
Irma was cooking dinner; in the meantime, Mario read the news-
    paper.
Jane took a nap; in the meantime, Bill was watching television.
Mario read the newspaper; in the meantime, Irma was cooking
    dinner.

Two other connecting words are used to describe more complex chronological relationships: the two-place connectors *since* and *until*.

*Since* is used when you wish to write about two events: the first event happened, then the other event began and has continued to the present time. Consider the following pairs of sentences:

We left Puerto Rico. From that time to the present, we have
    lived in New York.

Cleveland was hit by a blizzard. From that time to the present, the governor of Ohio has been in Florida.

These sentences can be combined as follows:

Since we left Puerto Rico, we have lived in New York.
We have lived in New York since we left Puerto Rico.

Since Cleveland was hit by a blizzard, the governor of Ohio has been in Florida.
The governor of Ohio has been in Florida since Cleveland was hit by a blizzard.

*Until* is used when you wish to write about two events: the first event went on for a period of time in the past, but it stopped when something else happened. Consider the following sentences:

I took the bus to school every day. Then I bought a car and quit taking the bus.
Ruth played basketball. Then she broke her arm and quit playing basketball.

These sentences can be combined in the following ways:

I took the bus to school every day until I bought a car.
Until I bought a car, I took the bus to school every day.

Ruth played basketball until she broke her arm.
Until Ruth broke her arm, she played basketball.

To summarize what we've learned about sentence connectors for chronological order, there are two kinds of connectors: two-place connectors (*after, before, when, as, while, since, until*) and semicolon connectors (*subsequently, afterwards, in the meantime*). Because all these words have special meanings, you must be sure to use them in the right places. You must also be careful to punctuate the sentences correctly when you use them.

## Sentence-Combining Practice

➤ Use time sentence connectors to combine the following pairs of sentences in *at least* two ways.

1. Dennis dusted the furniture. Then he vacuumed the carpet.

_____

_____

2. Vivian was studying her English. At the same time, Sheila watched television.

_____

_____

3. Mike drove a car. Then he had an accident and quit driving.

_____

_____

4. My sister graduated from college in 1989. From that time to the present, she has worked for the *San Francisco Chronicle*.

_____

_____

5. Suzanne was playing basketball. At the same time, Dave was cleaning the house.

_____

_____

6. Gary raked the leaves. Then he carried them to the garbage can.

_____

_____

7. The girls played volleyball. Then their coach was fired, and they quit playing.

_____

_____

8. We had twenty inches of snow in two days. From that time to the present, all the schools have been closed.

_____

_____

9. Keith lost his balance. Right away, he knocked over a chair.

_____

_____

10. Debbie entered the house. Right away, she smelled gas.

_____

_____

## Sentence-Creating Practice

➤ Write ten sentences of your own in which you use time sentence connectors.

1. _____

_____

2. _____

_____

3. _____

_____

4. _____

_____

5. _____

_____

6. _____

_____

7. _____

_____

8. _____

_____

9. _____

_____

10. _____

_____

# 6   SENTENCE COMBINING: PUTTING IT TOGETHER

In this section, you will have an opportunity to use what you have learned in this chapter about sentence combining.

➤ On your own paper, take each group of sentences and combine them into one sentence. For some groups, you may wish to use relative pronouns. For others, you may want to use time sentence connectors. For still others, you may have to think a little about what you already know about writing sentences.

## AN UNUSUAL CLASS

1. I was a sophomore in college.
2. I had a strange experience in a linguistics class.

3. One morning the professor walked into the room.
4. The professor was very young.
5. The room was filled with students.
6. The students were sleepy.

7. He slammed his books on the desk.
8. The students jumped.

9. He walked to the blackboard.
10. It was covered with writing.

11. He looked for an eraser.
12. He didn't find one.
13. He erased the board with a Kleenex.

14. He picked up a piece of chalk.
15. The chalk was yellow.
16. Then he started to write something.
17. The chalk broke into two pieces.
18. The pieces were tiny.

19. The professor looked for another piece of chalk.
20. Right away, he found one.
21. He started writing again.

22. He wrote the words *The Phoneme.*
23. The chalk broke into two pieces.
24. The pieces were tiny.
25. He quit writing.

26. He looked for another piece of chalk.
27. He didn't find one.

28. He put down the chalk.
29. Then he picked up his books.
30. He walked out of the room.

31. The students sat there silently.
32. They were bewildered.
33. Then one student giggled.

34. All the students began to laugh.
35. Then they left the room to go get some coffee.

## 7   USING WHAT YOU HAVE LEARNED IN OTHER WRITING ASSIGNMENTS

Now that you're familiar with chronological order as a way of organizing your ideas, you need to learn how to apply what you've learned to writing assignments in other classes or on your job.

What writing assignments are likely to permit you to use chronological order? As a general rule, any time you are asked to write about "what happened," you can use chronological order. For instance, in a history class, if you were asked to write about what happened during a particular battle in the Second World War, you could use chronological order to organize your ideas. In a chemistry class, you might be asked to write about what happened when you performed an experiment. Again, time order would be useful. Finally, on your job, you might be asked to write about what happened when your department started using a new piece of equipment. The question, "What happened?" tells you that chronological order would be an appropriate way of organizing your ideas.

## Extra Writing Practice

➤ Think of a "what happened" question that you've heard someone ask recently at school or on the job. Then write out a brief answer to the question using chronological order.

# THREE

# COMPARISON AND CONTRAST

## 1   THE READERS' EXPECTATIONS: MAKING A POINT

All of us have known people who announce that they have something to tell us. Then they begin to talk and talk. At first, we assume that they will eventually get to the important point. If they don't tell us quickly, we become impatient and say, "Would you please tell me what is so important? What are you trying to say?" If they want us to keep listening, they will probably tell us right away what the important thing is. Otherwise, we may stop listening or say, "I'm sorry. I have to run now. Tell me some other time."

Just as listeners get impatient with speakers who talk around a subject, readers get impatient with writers who ramble. However, unlike listeners, readers cannot ask the writer to get to the point. They must either keep reading and hope that they will discover the writer's main purpose or stop reading the paper or book in disgust, thinking, "I've got better things to do with my time." If you, as a writer, want to make sure that your readers will continue reading what you have written, you must clearly show them that you have something specific to communicate. This brings us to our sixth guideline for good writing:

> *Guideline 6:* Good writing must have a point—a main idea that the writer wants to communicate. (In some textbooks, the *main idea* is called a *thesis.*)

To examine the concept of the *main idea*, let's begin with the compositions you have already written.

Let's think, for example, about the composition that you wrote in Chapter 1 about your most favorite or least favorite spot. When you wrote that assignment, you used a *main idea* even though you did not realize it at the time. In that composition, you expressed *your viewpoint* on the best place or the worst place to be—an opinion that was different from those of your classmates. As you did so, you presented a main idea, because *the main idea of a piece of writing always expresses the writer's viewpoint, or opinion, on a particular subject.* To use another example, in the composition that you wrote in Chapter 2 titled, "How to Be a Terrible _____," you expressed your viewpoint on your subject, based on your own experiences. If other people had been writing the essay, based on their experiences in life, they might have chosen details very different from yours.

So you've already used a main idea or thesis in your writing. You've already expressed your viewpoint or opinion on a subject.

## Journal Assignment

➤ All of us have days when we wish we had stayed in bed because every little thing that could go wrong did go wrong. Use the prewriting techniques you've learned to develop a list of details about events that can wreck a person's day. Write a short composition in which you organize those details using chronological order to describe "The Day I Should Have Stayed in Bed."

## 2   MAKING A POINT THROUGH COMPARISON AND CONTRAST

You can use many different kinds of main ideas in compositions. In this chapter and the next three, you will learn about four different kinds of main ideas that you can communicate to your reader when you write.

In this chapter we're going to concentrate on one of them: comparison and contrast. Although the phrase *comparison and contrast* may be unfamiliar to you, you already know the *concept* of comparison and contrast. In fact, each time you go shopping, you probably make use of comparison and contrast thinking. For example, when you go shopping for a new pair of jeans, you don't usually buy the first pair you see. Instead, you look at several pairs to examine their quality, style, and price. Before you make up your mind which pair you are going to buy, you discover both the similarities and differences among the jeans. When you look for similarities, you are using comparison; when you look for differences, you are using contrast.

Since you are familiar with comparison and contrast thinking, you are now ready to learn how to develop main ideas for comparison and contrast compositions.

Let's imagine that you have decided that you want to write about the similarities and differences between baseball and football. As you might expect, your first prewriting task will be to think about the two sports and make two lists—one of similarities and another of differences. When you write your lists, they might look something like the following:

## Similarities

1. Both sports are played outdoors, so the weather can be very important.
2. Both games make use of a ball that players throw and catch.
3. The teams are approximately the same size—nine for baseball and eleven for football.

## Differences

1. Baseball is a summer sport, but football is played in the fall and winter.
2. Baseball players don't play in bad weather, but football players do.
3. Baseball players seldom get hurt seriously, but football players often do.
4. In baseball, most of the players on the field stand around waiting for something to happen. In football, every player on the field works on every play.
5. Time is not important in baseball. A team that is twenty runs behind in the ninth inning still has a chance to win. In football, time is very important. A team that is twenty points behind with one minute left in the game cannot win.
6. In baseball, there are no tie games. In football, a game can end in a tie, which means that nobody wins.

After examining these two lists, you may conclude that, in your opinion, the two sports have a few similarities, but the differences between them are really very important. When you make that conclusion, you have decided that you are going to write a composition whose main idea is like the following one:

**Baseball and football have a few things in common, but the two sports are really very different.**

On the other hand, suppose you make a list of similarities and differences and find that, in your opinion, the similarities are perhaps even more important than the differences. What do you do then? You could use a main idea like the following one:

**Spring and fall are different in a few ways, but the two seasons really have a great deal in common.**

So, in a comparison and contrast composition, it is possible to use one of two kinds of main ideas:

1. _____and_____have a few things in common,

   but the two_____are really very different.

2. _____and_____are different in a few ways, but

   the two_____are really very similar.

You can use whichever main idea expresses *your* opinion.

## Journal Assignment

➤ Choose a few pairs of subjects that you could compare and contrast. (As you select your pairs of subjects, it is important that you choose two things that are similar in some ways and different in other ways.) For each pair of subjects, write down all the similarities and differences you can think of. Then develop a comparison and contrast main idea for each list of similarities and differences. If you have difficulty finding a topic, here are some possibilities:

   Two sports that you enjoy watching or participating in
   Two athletic teams that you are familiar with
   Two of your relatives
   Two of your friends
   Two schools that you have attended
   Two jobs that you have held
   Two pets that you have had
   Two houses or apartments that you have lived in

## 3   CONSIDERING THE READERS' NEEDS: READERS' SIGNPOSTS

In Chapter 1, when we first discussed the differences between speaking and writing, one major difference we investigated was the fact that the audience is physically present when we talk but not when we write. So far, we have concentrated on the ways a writer can respond to this problem. In this section, we are going to concentrate on the reader's situation, and as we do so, you will discover how you, as a writer, can make your reader's task easier.

Let's begin by considering what happens when you sit down to read an article in a newspaper or an assignment in a textbook. Your task as a reader is to learn what main ideas the writer is trying to communicate. Sometimes it is easy to understand the main ideas, but at other times it is very difficult.

There are many possible reasons why some assignments are more easily understood than others. Generally, if you know the vocabulary and the subject matter, the reading selection will be easy for you to understand. However, there are times when even a knowledge of both the vocabulary and the subject matter will not help you determine what the writer is trying to communicate. When this happens, it may be because the writer has failed to make use of what we are going to call *readers' signposts*.

To help you learn how readers' signposts work, let's consider signposts on streets and roads. Street signs usually either tell the traveler where the road is going (for instance, a highway sign that says "To San Francisco" or "To Miami") or they tell the traveler where he or she is right at the moment (for example, a sign on a street corner that says "Pacific St. and Maple Ave."). Readers' signposts have the same two uses. That is, they tell the readers where they *are going* in terms of ideas and where they *are* at a particular moment in the composition. In slightly different words, readers' signposts lead the readers through the composition. They help the readers keep track of their location in terms of the writer's ideas. They are so important that they provide the basis for our seventh guideline for good writing:

> *Guideline 7:* Good writing provides signposts to help the reader.

To help you see how readers' signposts work, we're now going to do a writing workshop exercise.

## Writing Workshop Exercise

➤ Read the compositions below in order to answer the following questions: (1) What is the main idea in each composition? (2) Which composition makes it easier for you to follow the writer's ideas? (3) In the composition that makes it easier, what are the signposts that tell the reader where he or she is going and where he or she is?

COMPOSITION 1: SPRING AND FALL

Spring is the season when trees go from leafless to bright green, and it's the season when tulips, crocuses, and daffodils leap out of the ground and begin to flower. In spring, everyone is excited and happy because winter has gone and won't return for months. Fall is the season when trees go from bright green to leafless, and it's the season when the only flowers left are chrysanthemums. In fall, people get very wistful because summer has gone and won't return for months.

In both fall and spring, the weather is moderate--not too hot and not too cold. We neither burn nor freeze. Both spring and fall are seasons when things in nature change dramatically. The trees go from leafless to bright green and vice versa. The temperature goes from cold to warm and vice versa. In spring and fall, we are very aware of how things change in nature and of how things change in our lives. Both spring and fall are next to winter, the season when nature seems dead. Because spring and autumn are so close in time to the season of death, they are the times when we are most aware of the life cycle--of its beginning and its end.

COMPOSITION 2: SPRING AND FALL

For most people, spring and fall are two completely different seasons; however, I think that the two seasons really have more in common than most people realize.

Let me begin by admitting that it is obvious that the two seasons are not identical. Spring is the season when trees go from leafless to bright green, and it's the season when tulips, crocuses, and daffodils leap out of the ground and begin to flower. In spring, everyone is excited and happy because winter has gone and won't return for months. On the other hand, fall is the season when trees go from bright green to leafless, and it's the season when the only flowers left are chrysanthemums. Also, in fall, people get very wistful because summer has gone and won't return for months.

However, in spite of these real differences, fall and spring do have a great deal in common. For one thing, the weather is moderate--not too hot and not too cold; as a result, we neither burn nor freeze. In addition, both spring and autumn are seasons when things in nature change dramatically. One example that shows this has already been mentioned; namely, the way the trees go from leafless to bright green and vice versa. Another example is the way the temperature changes from cold to warm and vice versa. As a result of these changes, in spring and fall we are very aware of how things change in nature and how things change in our lives. One final similarity concerns the fact that both spring and fall are next to winter, the season when nature seems dead. Because spring and autumn are so close in time to the season of death, they are the times when we are most aware of the life cycle--of its beginning and its end.

Thus, although spring and fall may seem to be different when we think about them casually, they prove to be rather similar if we think about them carefully.

# 4  PARAGRAPHING AND COMPARISON AND CONTRAST

Before you write your comparison and contrast composition, we need to consider two things: paragraphing and the use of readers' signposts.

As far as paragraphing is concerned, if you use the definition we proposed in Chapter 2, *that a paragraph is a section of a composition that deals with a particular point,* you can guess that a comparison and contrast composition could easily become a four-paragraph composition. The point of the first paragraph would be to introduce the main idea. The two middle paragraphs would have as their purposes the discussion of similarities and differences, and the fourth paragraph would be designed to conclude the composition. Although this is not the only possible way to organize a comparison-contrast essay, it is one that is quite easy to use.

Now let's consider readers' signposts. In Section 3, you learned about two kinds of signposts—those that tell your reader where you are going in the composition and those that tell your reader where you are at a particular point in the composition. When you present the main idea of your essay, you provide the reader with a signpost that tells where the essay is going. But what, you may be wondering, are the signposts that tell the reader where you *are* at a particular point in the composition?

One such signpost that may already be familiar to you is called the *topic sentence of a paragraph.* If you've ever studied paragraphs before, you've learned that many paragraphs include a sentence (often, though not always, the first sentence) that summarizes the particular point of the essay that will be developed in that paragraph. For instance, in Composition 2, "Spring and Fall," the first sentence in the second paragraph tells the reader that the writer will be discussing the differences that the writer has mentioned in the main idea. The first sentence in the third paragraph announces that the writer is now going to consider the similarities. Both topic sentences remind the reader of the main idea: they tell the readers where they are with respect to the main idea.

As you write your comparison and contrast composition, you will want to use topic sentences that will help the reader to follow your ideas. Here are some topic sentences that may be useful to you in your composition:

First, let's examine the similarities.
Now, let's consider the differences.
First, let's discuss the differences.
Now, let's examine the similarities.

You will develop the topic sentences of the paragraphs by providing details explaining the similarities and differences.

Topic sentences are one kind of signpost that tells the reader where you are in the composition. Another kind of signpost that does the same thing is the *conclusion signal.* This kind of signpost lets the reader know that the end of the composition is coming. In written English, several phrases can be used to announce that a conclusion is coming:

In conclusion,      To summarize,      Thus,
To conclude,        In summary,

If you use phrases like these to begin the final paragraph in your composition, you let the reader know that you are bringing the composition to an end.

## COMPOSITION ASSIGNMENT

Examine the comparison and contrast main ideas that you developed for various topics in the journal assignment at the conclusion of Section 2. Choose one main idea that you would like to write about, and develop that idea into a composition. Be sure to use readers' signposts as you write the essay, and be sure to proofread the essay before you hand it in.

## 5   SENTENCE COMBINING IN WRITTEN ENGLISH: COMPARISON AND CONTRAST

In this section, we will consider some more sentence connectors that are often useful, especially when you write about comparison and contrast.

Let's begin by considering the following sentences, which describe similarities between two people:

Jane and her mother are very courageous. They are totally honest with other people.

There are several ways of combining these sentences using sentence connectors. One way that you already know is through the use of the word *and*. For example:

Jane and her mother are very courageous, and they are totally honest with other people.

Four other sentence connectors are often used in written English to combine sentences of comparison. The following examples show this:

Jane and her mother are very courageous; also, they are totally honest with other people.
Jane and her mother are very courageous; in addition, they are totally honest with other people.
Jane and her mother are very courageous; moreover, they are totally honest with other people.

> Jane and her mother are very courageous; furthermore, they are totally honest with other people.

As you can tell from these examples, the words *also, in addition, moreover,* and *furthermore* are all semicolon connectors, which, as you'll remember, require a semicolon before them and a comma after them. But the word *and,* when it is used to join two sentences of comparison, is punctuated differently. It is used with a *comma* before it and no punctuation mark after it. To help you remember the punctuation rule for *and* as a sentence connector, we will call *and* a *comma connector*.

Now let's turn our attention to sentences that describe differences. Consider the following sentences showing a contrast between two people:

> Jim Murphy is very honest. His son is a thief.

You already know how to combine these sentences by using the word *but*:

> Jim Murphy is very honest, but his son is a thief.

As you can tell from this example, the word *but* belongs to the category of words that we call comma connectors. There is another comma connector that can be used to link these two sentences, although you may not be familiar with it because it is not very common in spoken English. This comma connector is the word *yet*, and it is used in the following way:

> Jim Murphy is very honest, yet his son is a thief.

There are other possible ways of connecting these sentences using different kinds of connectors. You can use the semicolon connectors *however, nevertheless,* and *on the other hand*. These are often used in written English to express a contrast. For example:

> Jim Murphy is very honest; however, his son is a thief.
> Jim Murphy is very honest; nevertheless, his son is a thief.
> Jim Murphy is very honest; on the other hand, his son is a thief.

You can also use the two-place connector *although*:

> Although Jim Murphy is very honest, his son is a thief.
> Jim Murphy is very honest although his son is a thief.

So far, we have only considered how to use these sentence connectors when comparing and contrasting two different people or things. However, these connectors may also be used when discussing two different qualities of one person or thing. Consider the following sentences:

Jane's boyfriend is very handsome. He is very intelligent.

In these sentences, the writer is describing two different qualities of Jane's boyfriend. Because both qualities are good ones for a person to have, they are similar. It is therefore possible to use *comparison* connectors to combine these sentences. For example:

Jane's boyfriend is very handsome; moreover, he is very intelligent.
Jane's boyfriend is very handsome; in addition, he is very intelligent.

But suppose the writer wanted to combine the following sentences:

Joan's boyfriend is very handsome. He is very stupid.

In these sentences, one of the qualities is good, but the other is bad. Because the two qualities are *different, contrast* connectors would be used to combine these sentences:

Joan's boyfriend is very handsome; however, he is very stupid.
Joan's boyfriend is very handsome; on the other hand, he is very stupid.

Before we leave the subject of comparison and contrast connectors, we need to consider one other matter. As you have learned in this section, many comparison and contrast connectors belong to the category of semicolon connectors (connectors that are punctuated with a semicolon before them and a comma after them). However, it is also possible to punctuate these connectors in a slightly different way, as the following examples show:

Jane's boyfriend is very handsome. Moreover, he is very intelligent.
Jane's boyfriend is very handsome. In addition, he is very intelligent.

In these sentences, the sentence connectors do not combine two sentences into one sentence. Instead, the connectors are used to show that the *ideas* in two *separate* sentences are very closely connected. So the sentence connectors are still working as sentence connectors even though there are two separate sentences.

You can use this method of punctuating *moreover* and *in addition* with all the semicolon connectors in written English. To illustrate, look at the following examples from Chapter 2 as well as from this section:

Mark washed the car. Afterwards, he cooked dinner.
Mark washed the car. Subsequently, he cooked dinner.
Bill was watching television. In the meantime, Jane took a nap.

Joan's boyfriend is very handsome. However, he is very stupid.
Jim Murphy is very honest. Nevertheless, his son is a thief.

## Sentence-Combining Practice

➤ Combine the following pairs of sentences using the sentence connectors you were introduced to in this section. Before you choose a connector, decide whether the two sentences describe a comparison or a contrast. Then try to combine each pair of sentences in two different ways. By the end of the section, you should have used all the sentence connectors.

1. Rita likes classical music. Her sister prefers rock music.

_____

_____

2. Jeremy plans to go to medical school. His brother was a high school dropout.

_____

_____

3. Roberto and his father like to go fishing. They enjoy backpacking.

_____

_____

4. Jack and Sue are good bridge players. They are excellent chess players.

_____

_____

5. My mother loves to dance. My father would rather watch football.

_____

_____

6. Cynthia and Gloria want to be lawyers. They hope to go to Harvard Law School.

_____

_____

7. Steve's girlfriend is very beautiful. She is very intelligent.

_____

_____

8. Martha and Henry are excellent swimmers. They are good volleyball players.

_____

_____

9. The public schools must accept any student. The Catholic schools can refuse to take problem students.

_____

_____

10. My sociology professor expects students to work too hard. She really likes the students in her class.

_____

_____

11. My biology professor and my chemistry professor are very boring. They give tests that almost no one can pass.

_____

_____

12. Elena plays the piano beautifully. She cannot sing very well.

_____

_____

## Sentence–Creating Practice

➤ Write five sentences of your own in which you use comparison connectors. Then write five sentences in which you use contrast connectors. (Try to avoid using the connectors *and* and *but*.)

1. _____

_____

2. _____

_____

3. _____

_____

4. _____

_____

5. _____

_____

1. _____

_____

2. _____

_____

3. _____

_____

4. _____

_____

5. _____

_____

## 6  SENTENCE COMBINING: PUTTING IT TOGETHER

➤ On your own paper, combine the sentences in the groups using the various connectors you have learned to use. For some of the sentences, you will want to use comparison connectors or contrast connectors. For others, you will want to use some other way of combining the sentences. In addition, break this selection into paragraphs and add readers' signposts as you would if you were writing it as a composition.

### BASEBALL AND FOOTBALL

1. My mother doesn't know much about football and baseball.
2. She thinks the two sports are very similar.

3. I have played both sports.
4. I know the two sports are really very different.

5. Baseball is played outdoors.
6. Football is played outdoors.
7. The weather can be very important.

8. Baseball makes use of a ball.
9. Players throw the ball.
10. Players catch the ball.
11. Football makes use of a ball.
12. Players throw the ball.
13. Players catch the ball.

14. In baseball, the players try to score points.
15. In football, the players try to score points.

16. Baseball players don't spend the whole game on the field.
17. Football players don't spend the whole game on the field.

18. The weather is very important in both games.
19. Baseball teams don't have to play on rainy days.
20. Football teams have to play on rainy days.
21. Football teams have to play in the sleet.
22. Football teams have to play in the snow.
23. Football players sometimes get wet and cold.

24. In baseball, most of the nine players on the field stand around.
25. They are waiting for the batter to hit the ball.
26. In football, all eleven players work on every play.
27. No one waits for something to happen.

28. In baseball, players seldom knock each other down.
29. In football, on every play someone gets knocked down.

30. In baseball, players seldom get seriously hurt.
31. In every football game, there is one player.
32. He is hurt very seriously.
33. He has to be carried off the field.

34. In baseball, there is no time clock.
35. A team is twenty runs behind in the ninth inning.
36. The team still has a chance to win the game.
37. In football, time is very important.
38. A team is twenty points behind.
39. There is one minute left in the game.
40. The team cannot win the game.

41. Every baseball game has a winner and a loser.
42. You know that one team will be happy at the end of the game.
43. In football, some games end in a tie.
44. Both teams may go home frustrated and angry.

45. Football and baseball have a few similarities.
46. They are truly different sports.

47. Baseball players have an easy life.
48. Football players have a terrible life.
49. That's why I have quit playing football.

# 7   USING WHAT YOU HAVE LEARNED IN OTHER WRITING ASSIGNMENTS

In Chapter 2, you discovered that many writing assignments can be organized using chronological order. In this section, we will explore ways of applying what you've learned in this chapter to writing assignments you are given.

You can use comparison and contrast to organize your ideas any time you are asked to write about two things. For instance, during an exam in history class, you might be asked to discuss the American Revolution of 1776 and the French Revolution of 1789, and you could use comparison and contrast to organize your essay. In a literature class, you might be asked to write a paper examining two characters in a novel, and you could organize your paper by presenting first the similarities and then the differences between the two characters. In political science, if you were asked to discuss the U.S. Congress and your state legislature, comparison and contrast would be an appropriate organizational pattern.

At this point, you may be wondering if comparison and contrast will be a useful organization pattern for you only while you are in school. So we need to consider other uses of the pattern that occur in the nonacademic world.

Almost any job you may ever hold will at some point deal with comparison and contrast. For example, if you're working for a corporation, your boss might ask you to write a report on two computer systems that your company might buy, and you could use comparison and contrast as a way of organizing your ideas. If you were working in a school, you might be asked to evaluate two different series of textbooks that your school system was thinking about adopting, and comparison and contrast would be an appropriate way to organize your report.

Any club or church that you belong to will, from time to time, be investigating "two things": two potential locations for the annual picnic, two potential ministers or music directors, two potential sources of T-shirts. A discussion of similarities and differences would be an appropriate format for your report.

### Extra Writing Practice

➤ For the next few days, be on the lookout for examples of comparison and contrast in your life at home, at school, and on the job. Keep a record of those pairs of topics that could be discussed using comparison and contrast. Then choose one, and write a comparison and contrast essay on that subject.

# FOUR

## DEFENDING A CHOICE

## 1 WRITING TO DISCOVER IDEAS: DISCOVERY PROCEDURES

In Chapter 1, we talked about two reasons for liking to write: (1) writing is a way to tell other people something you have learned from your experience, because you've lived a life that is completely different from the lives of all your classmates and teachers; and (2) writing is a way to discover new thoughts and new ideas. In this section, we're going to focus on that second reason.

Sometimes writers are lucky. They know exactly what topic they want to write about and what they want to say about that topic. At other times, however, they are not at all sure what they want to say. When experienced writers are in this situation, they sometimes use what are called *discovery procedures*, or ways of investigating a topic to discover a main idea that will give them something to say.

Although you may not have been aware of it, you used a *discovery procedure* in Chapter 3 as you were learning how to write a comparison and contrast composition. You were introduced to a way of investigating two subjects in order to discover a main idea that you could use in a composition. You examined the two in order to determine whether there were more similarities or more differences, and you then developed a main idea for a composition in which you presented the point of view you had discovered. As you were working on the essay, you may have realized that the two subjects you were examining had many more similarities than you had expected to find, or vice versa. With this discovery, you experienced one of the joys of writing.

If you haven't yet experienced that pleasure, you will get an opportunity to do so now as you use what you already know about comparison and contrast to investigate a subject you perhaps have never thought seriously about before—the subject of how *you yourself* have changed and how you've stayed the same as you've matured.

To prepare you for this experience, we're going to do a writing workshop exercise.

## Writing Workshop Exercise

➤ Read the composition below, and answer the following questions: (1) What is the main idea of the composition? (2) What general kinds of human characteristics does the writer consider in the essay? (3) As you read the essay, what things in it make you think about your own life?

MYSELF THEN AND NOW

On the day before Thanksgiving, I went down to my parents' basement to get the roasting pan we were going to use to cook the turkey the next day. As I was walking toward the cabinet where my mother kept the roasting pan, I passed the cedar chest she had bought before she married. On an impulse, I opened the chest and found a photograph album containing pictures of me when I was a child. As I gazed at the pictures, my mind kept moving back and forth from past to present as I thought about the person I once was and the person I am now.

When I first looked at the pictures, I felt that I now am a person so different from that child in the past that it seemed impossible we could be the same person. For one thing, my appearance has changed dramatically. When I was a child, I had straight, light blonde hair that was so long it touched my waist. Now I have short brown hair that is very curly, thanks to a permanent. Then I wore glasses, but now I have contact lenses. As a child, I was the tallest girl in my class; however, I stopped growing when I was eleven, so now I am one of the shortest women in the school. And of course, my body has changed from a girl's body to a woman's body.

Not only has my physical appearance changed, but also many things about my behavior have changed. When I was a child, I could do cartwheels, handstands, and splits. Today I can barely touch my toes. When I was in elementary school, I was active in the school athletic program, playing softball, volleyball, and basketball; however, today, whenever I feel the urge to get some exercise, I lie down and wait for the urge to go away. Thus, I have changed from an active person to a lazier one. I have also become more self-conscious as I have grown older. When I was little, I loved to perform in front of an audience. I enjoyed being in school plays, and I loved to be in the recitals that my ballet teacher would present. Today I get nervous whenever I have to answer a question in class even if I know that I have the right answer. When I was a child, I had no trouble carrying on a conversation with anyone, but now whenever I meet someone new, I can't think of anything to say, so I stand there, looking like a dummy who is waiting for a ventriloquist.

The more I thought about the differences between myself now and the girl I was then, the more I thought I was looking at a stranger. Was it possible that the child in those pictures and I were truly the same person?

Then I noticed one picture that was taken when I wasn't aware that anyone was watching me. In that picture, I was lost in thought, reading a book. As I gazed at that picture, I began to think about those things that haven't changed. I have always loved to read books. When I was a child, my mother would yell at me to do some chores around the house, but I wouldn't hear her because I was lost in a book. The same thing happens today. For another similarity, I've always loved to write. When I was a child, I wrote poetry. As an adult, I write entries in my journal, but always I have written.

The more I thought about my childhood, the more I realized that inside my mind, I am still very much the same per-

son. For instance, I still think many of the same thoughts.
As a child, I was afraid of monsters that might be lurking in
the dark. Today I am afraid of monsters that are lurking in
the future, like unemployment, nuclear war, or environmental
pollution. When I was little, I thought that adults were the
most peculiar creatures on earth because they were always doing and saying the strangest things. I still feel the same
way about adults.

In conclusion, while my physical appearance and my behavior in public have changed, the person I am in private has
not changed. In certain respects, the girl I used to be is a
stranger, but in other respects, she is someone I know very
well.

## Journal Assignment

➤ Write a few pages in which you consider the child you were between the
ages of seven and ten and the adult you are now. Examine the ways you
have changed and the ways you have stayed the same as you have grown
older. As you're planning the essay, you may want to focus on the following
kinds of human characteristics: physical appearance, behavior toward others,
emotions, interests, thoughts, and so on. Organize your ideas using comparison and contrast.

## 2   THINKING ABOUT DEFENDING AN OPINION

Whenever a writer selects a topic and develops a main idea for a composition,
he or she must then find some way to present the idea to the reader in a way that
will make the reader willing to pay attention.

As you learned in Chapter 3, the *main idea* of an essay expresses the writer's
*viewpoint* or *opinion* on a topic. As you already know from your experiences in the
world, different people have different opinions. Some opinions involve minor
differences, such as whether or not we like coffee, tennis, and English class. Some

of these opinions involve major differences—for example, how we feel about abortion, whether we consider ourselves Republicans or Democrats or Independents, or how we feel about the Middle East.

Because not everyone holds the same opinions, you as a writer cannot be sure that your readers will agree with the ideas you are trying to communicate. How, then, can you make sure that your readers will be willing to pay attention to your ideas? Although this question has no easy answers, you can try to convince your readers that you have spent some time thinking seriously about your views. If your readers believe that you have done serious thinking on the subject, then they will be more willing to respect your views, even though they may disagree with them. We can sum this idea up as our eighth guideline for good writing:

> *Guideline 8:* Good writers understand that they must convince the reader that they have thought seriously about the ideas they are trying to communicate.

Writers convince the reader that they have thought seriously about their opinions by trying to find good reasons to answer the question "Why do you hold that opinion?"—good reasons and concrete details that help the reader understand the writers' viewpoints. How do they do this? In this section and the next two, we will consider some techniques that writers use. First, we'll look at two essays in which writers who strongly disagree with each other have tried to convince the reader that they have thought seriously about their subject. These essays will help you understand how writers can assure the reader they have good reasons for believing as they do, no matter what their opinions may be.

## Writing Workshop Exercise

➤ Read the two compositions below, and answer the following questions about each essay: (1) What is the main idea? (2) What reasons does the writer present to defend the main idea? (3) What details does the writer use to develop the reasons into paragraphs? (4) Does the writer convince you that he or she has thought seriously about the opinion defended in the essay?

COMPOSITION 1: CATS VS. DOGS

Some people argue that the world is made up of two kinds of people: those who prefer cats and those who prefer dogs. I belong to the latter group. I think that dogs make better pets than cats do.

First of all, dogs make better pets than cats because dogs are much more intelligent. They can be taught to do all kinds of things. For instance, you can teach a dog to sit still when you command him to, and he will remain motionless until you tell him to move. A dog can learn to sit up on his hind legs and beg for food. A dog can also learn to play games like "fetch the stick" or "chase the ball." In fact, dogs are so smart that they can learn all the things they need to know in order to serve as "seeing eyes" for the blind. In contrast, cats cannot be taught to do anything except use the litter box.

Because dogs are so intelligent, they are extremely helpful to their owners. A dog will fetch the newspaper or your slippers. Dogs will bark to let you know when someone is coming to your door. As a result, the smallest dog can scare away criminals, who hear a barking dog but can't be sure whether they hear a miniature poodle or a German shepherd, so they leave your house or apartment alone and go to an unprotected home. For another example, a dog will awaken you to let you know if something in the house is burning; as a result, a dog can truly save your life. On the other hand, the only thing a cat is good for is to sit and look pretty.

Finally, dogs are much more affectionate companions than cats are. A dog will come whenever you call him and will let you pet him whenever you feel like it. Cats never come when you call them, and they expect to be petted only when <u>they</u> feel like it, as opposed to when you feel like it. A dog will go for a walk with you; however, as soon as you let a cat out of the house, it runs off wherever it wants to go. Finally,

when you've been away from home for a while, a dog is so happy
to see you that he wags his tail and licks you. A cat simply
looks at you as if to say, "Have you been away? I didn't notice."

In conclusion, if you want a not very bright, useless,
unaffectionate pet, get a cat. On the other hand, if you want
an intelligent, useful, affectionate pet, then join the ranks
of those who know that dogs are truly "man's best friends."


COMPOSITION 2: DOGS VS. CATS


Some people argue that the world is made up of two kinds
of people: those who prefer dogs and those who prefer cats. I
belong to the latter group. I think that cats make better
pets than dogs do.

Cats are more intelligent than dogs. For instance, a
kitten can be toilet trained in 30 minutes. All the owner has
to do is put the kitten in the litter box and show it how to
use its paws to dig in the litter. Dog owners must work for
days and sometimes weeks to toilet train a puppy. For another
example, a cat is smart enough to figure out how to eat "all
the good stuff" on a fish without swallowing even the tiniest
bone, but a dog can't even discover how to get chicken off the
bone without getting seriously hurt. Finally, cats are too
smart to learn foolish little tricks. They know their owners
will love them even if they refuse to fetch a stick, but dogs
think they must work to get their owner's love.

Cats are much more independent than dogs. A cat can be
left for a couple of days and survive quite nicely. All the
owner must do is leave a clean litter box and plenty of dry
food and water, and the cat will take care of all its needs.

However, a dog cannot be left alone for more than five or six hours. For one thing, it will make a terrible mess in the house if the owners don't get home in time to take it for a walk. Moreover, if a dog is given enough food for two days, it will eat all the food right away and go hungry if the owners don't return soon.

Because cats are so independent, they make their owners' lives much easier. If a cat owner's boss asks him or her to work overtime, the employee can say, "Yes," without worrying that the cat needs to be taken outdoors or that the poor cat will get so hungry that it will start chewing on the furniture. The owner can even go away for a long weekend, knowing that the cat will survive quite nicely. But a dog owner is a slave to the dog, who can never be left alone very long.

In summary, if you want an animal that will make you its slave, then get a dog. On the other hand, if you want a pet that will give you a little freedom, then join the ranks of those who appreciate our feline friends.

## 3   AN INTRODUCTION TO VERBAL REASONING

In this section, we will address the question of how you can convince your reader that you have thought seriously about the opinions you are presenting.

Perhaps the most important thing you can do is to make sure that you really *have* thought seriously about your ideas. You can do that by engaging in an activity called *verbal reasoning*, an activity you already know a great deal about.

Any time you ask the question "Why?" and search for answers to it, you are engaging in verbal reasoning. For instance, when you were a child, you participated in verbal reasoning with your parents when you asked them, "Why do I have to go to bed now?" or "Why can't I play in the street?" As you grew older, you engaged in the same activity all by yourself when you found your own answers to "Why?" questions in order to convince your mother or father to allow you to do such things as stay out until after midnight. So you've been engaging in verbal reasoning for most of your life.

You've also learned that some reasons are better than other reasons. For instance, suppose you once asked your mother why you could not stay out after ten at night. If she told you that you couldn't just because she said so, you may have obeyed her, but you probably felt that she didn't have a good reason for making that rule. On the other hand, if she told you that you needed to get your sleep for school the next day, you may not have agreed, but you at least had to admit that she had thought the matter out.

Finally, you know that the more good reasons someone can give you in answer to the question "Why?" the more likely you are to conclude that the person has really thought seriously about the matter. So you are already familiar with the kind of verbal reasoning that you need to engage in if you want to convince your reader that your opinions are the product of a great deal of serious thought.

Now you need to apply what you know about verbal reasoning to the problem of discovering good reasons and details that you can use to defend an opinion when you're writing.

Suppose you want to write a composition with the following main idea: "My sociology professor is a better teacher than my history professor is." As you think about your topic, one prewriting technique you can use is to keep asking yourself, "Why do I feel this way?" In response, you might come up with the following reasons: (1) The sociology professor shows much greater fairness in her grading. (2) The sociology lectures are interesting, but the history lectures are boring. (3) The history professor expects too much work from you, but the sociology professor has reasonable expectations.

The next step is to look for details you can use to convince the reader that your reasons are good ones. To find those details, you must once again ask yourself, "Why do I feel this way?" For instance, do you think the history professor grades unfairly because you failed the last test? Or do you think he grades too harshly because he asks questions on tests that he hasn't discussed in the lectures and the textbook doesn't answer them either? Do you think the sociology professor grades fairly because she gives everyone A's or B's or because her tests cover the material she has presented in the lectures?

Do you think the history lectures are boring because you don't understand everything the professor says, or because he spends all his time looking down at his lecture notes and talking in a very low voice while most of the students fall asleep? Do you think the sociology lectures are interesting because she shows entertaining movies and tells a lot of jokes, or because she shows you why sociology is important to your life?

As you ask yourself about your feelings, you should begin to discover whether or not the reasons for your feelings are valid, whether you can provide specific details that will convince your reader that you have thought seriously about the question, and whether your reader can, therefore, respect your opinion.

If you discover that you don't have good reasons, then you need to find another topic to write about. However, if your reasons have substance, then you can develop the topic into a composition that will support your opinion. Your reasons can be used as topic sentences for paragraphs. You can develop the topic sentences by providing the concrete details that will assure your reader that you have good reasons for feeling the way you do.

## Journal Assignment

➤ Think about the compositions you read in Section 2. Then compile a list of possible pairs of topics that you might want to develop into a composition in which you explain why you prefer one object or activity over another. When you've written your list, practice *verbal reasoning* to see if you can come up with some good reasons to defend your choice, and write down the reasons you can think of. If you have difficulty finding topics, here are some ideas that you may find helpful:

| | |
|---|---|
| two jobs | two bosses |
| two sports | two friends |
| two teachers | two household chores |
| two holidays | two houses or apartments |
| two cars | eating fast food versus cooking meals |
| two games | |

## 4   A DISCOVERY PROCEDURE FOR FINDING REASONS

Writers sometimes encounter some difficulty in coming up with reasons to use to defend a choice. When professional writers have this problem, they sometimes just quit writing for the day and hope that ideas will come the next day. However, when they have a deadline to meet, they have to find something to say in a hurry. In this situation, they can use *discovery procedures* to help them find good reasons.

Good writers have a large stock of discovery procedures, and in time you too will develop lots of these techniques. For now, we're going to focus on a technique called *factor analysis*, one discovery procedure you can use whenever you have difficulty finding good reasons to present to defend your opinion.

When you use factor analysis, you investigate the main idea you want to write about by asking a series of questions that can help you find ideas you can use to defend your opinion. Specifically, you ask *six* kinds of questions: (1) economic, (2) medical or physical, (3) environmental, (4) educational or mental, (5) psychological or emotional, and (6) social.

To see how you can use these questions, let's look at each kind in detail. First, let's consider *economic issues*. Can you find reasons to defend your point of view that relate to financial considerations—to earning, saving, or spending money? For instance, if you were explaining why you would rather ride a bike to school than drive a car, you could write about why owning a bike is much less expensive than owning a car. If you wanted to explain your preference for card games like bridge or pinochle over computer games, you could talk about the low cost of a deck of cards versus the higher cost of a computer game.

Second, let's examine *medical or physical reasons*. Can you defend your main idea by showing how people will benefit medically or physically if they listen to you? For example, if you were writing about bicycles versus cars, you might argue that people who ride bicycles get exercise that strengthens their leg muscles and also improves their cardiovascular systems. People who drive cars get no exercise at all. If you were explaining why you would rather play soccer than football, you could talk about all the terrible ways football players injure their bodies and about the terrific aerobic exercise soccer players get as they run up and down the field.

*Environmental reasons*, as you might expect, refer to ways we can create or avoid creating pollution in the world around us. Suppose you wanted to justify your preference for bicycles over cars. You could discuss the problem of air pollution that is caused by automobile exhaust, as well as the problem of farmland that is lost because of the need for parking lots. If you were defending card games over computer games, you could talk about how computers require electricity that must come from nuclear power or coal, both of which pollute the environment. On the other hand, cards don't require any electricity at all.

*Educational or mental reasons* concern ways of helping or harming the mental growth of individuals. If you were explaining why you would rather play chess than baseball, you could write about the intellectual skills a person must develop in order to be a good chess player. However, baseball only requires a person to develop the body. If you were defending your desire to take public transportation to school rather than to drive a car, you could talk about all the school assignments you complete on the way home because you aren't driving.

When we consider *psychological or emotional issues,* we're looking for things that cause positive or negative feelings. For instance, if you were writing about public transportation versus cars, you could talk about how tense and irritable people become as they're driving home during rush hour because of all the crazy drivers on the road. If you were writing about why you would rather go hiking than play basketball, you could talk about how relaxing it is to hike because you aren't worrying about making a mistake that might cost your team the game.

*Social reasons* are those that relate to improving or hurting our social relationships with other people. For instance, you might prefer playing basketball over hiking because basketball is a good way to meet new people and make new friends, but hiking is a very solitary activity. If you were defending card games like bridge and pinochle over computer games, you could argue that you learn about how to work effectively with people when you're playing card games that require you to cooperate with a partner. You don't learn to work well with people by playing with a machine.

Now that you've become familiar with the six kinds of reasons, you need to know two other things before you practice factor analysis. First, you should be aware that when you're using the "factors," you may discover that some of them don't apply to your main idea at all. For instance, if you're writing about why you would rather play cards than play computer games, you may not be able to come up with physical or medical reasons to defend your choice, or you may not be able to find emotional or psychological reasons. When you discover that a particular factor isn't useful, just forget about it. Second, if you cannot come up with two or three reasons to defend your main idea when you're using factor analysis, then perhaps you need to consider writing about some other main idea.

## COMPOSITION ASSIGNMENT

Write a composition in which you defend a choice between two things. Each of the body paragraphs should begin with a topic sentence that presents one of your reasons, and each paragraph should provide concrete details that develop the topic sentence. These details should help the reader understand exactly how the two things differ. As you're prewriting, try using factor analysis as a discovery procedure to help you find reasons and details.

## 5  SENTENCE COMBINING IN WRITTEN ENGLISH: GENERALIZATIONS AND EXAMPLES

Before we consider the sentence connectors that can be used to present your reasons and details, we need to discuss two concepts that are essential to the process of verbal reasoning: generalizations and specific examples. Whenever you form an opinion about anything, you make a generalization based on specific examples in your experience.

A *generalization* is a conclusion you make after a number of experiences. For example, you plan to go to a movie with your friend Betty. When you go to her house to pick her up, she isn't ready, so you have to wait twenty minutes until she is dressed. Two weeks later, she tells you that she will pick you up at 7:00 to drive you to a basketball game; however, she doesn't arrive until 7:45. If you have a few more similar experiences, you will draw a conclusion that Betty is almost always late. In other words, you will make a generalization about Betty based on specific examples in your experience.

It is possible to make a generalization about a particular individual, and sometimes about a group of people as well (although we must be careful not to make insulting or degrading statements about groups based on their race, gender, religion, and so on). For example, we might generalize that Marines are tough or that professional football players are very aggressive. We might also make generalizations about other kinds of groups: fast-food restaurants serve unnutritious meals, or small cars are very economical. All these generalizations can be made after we have lots of specific experiences. They are based on *specific examples*.

You can use those specific examples as concrete details in your writing to convince your reader that you have good reasons for feeling the way you do. When you want to give such examples in your writing, you can use two sentence connectors: the semicolon connectors *for example* and *for instance*. To understand how to use them, consider the following sentences:

| **Generalization** | **Specific Example** |
| --- | --- |
| Dogs can be taught to do all kinds of things. | You can teach a dog to sit still when you command him to. |

These sentences can be combined into one long sentence that makes it clear to the reader that you are providing a generalization and an example. Let's look at the following sentences:

Dogs can be taught to do all kinds of things; for example, you
   can teach a dog to sit still when you command him to.
Dogs can be taught to do all kinds of things; for instance, you can
   teach a dog to sit still when you command him to.

As you learned in Chapter 3, with semicolon connectors, it is possible to use separate sentences, punctuating them as the following examples illustrate:

Dogs can be taught to do all kinds of things. For example, you
   can teach a dog to sit still when you command him to.
Dogs can be taught to do all kinds of things. For instance, you
   can teach a dog to sit still when you command him to.

This particular use of semicolon connectors is very common in written English and is especially useful when a writer wants to give a long example to support a generalization, as in the following paragraph:

```
     Some people on welfare really need it. For instance, my
neighbor's husband died and left her with three preschool
```

children. She did not want to go on welfare, so she got a job
as a secretary, and she hired a baby-sitter. Soon she discovered that the baby-sitter wasn't taking good care of the
children. When she tried to find a really good baby-sitter,
she found that she couldn't afford to support her family and
pay a good baby-sitter on the salary she was making. So she
had to quit work in order to make sure that her children received good care. A person like that deserves welfare.

### Sentence-Combining Practice

➤ Listed below are pairs of sentences. In each pair one sentence is the
generalization, and the other gives a specific example. Using *for example* and
*for instance*, combine the two sentences, or use the connectors to show that
two separate sentences are closely connected. (Make sure that the generalization comes first.)

1. The game of bridge helps you improve your powers of concentration. You
   must pay attention to every card that is played so that you can outsmart your
   opponents.

   _____

   _____

   _____

2. Jogging is good for your cardiovascular system. When you run for thirty
   minutes, your heart muscles get stronger as the heart works hard to pump blood
   to all parts of your body.

   _____

   _____

   _____

3. The only equipment you need to play soccer is a ball that you can buy for a few dollars. Soccer is an inexpensive way to get exercise.

_____

_____

_____

4. The exhaust fumes from cars contain carbon monoxide. Driving a car to school contributes to air pollution.

_____

_____

_____

5. When I play the guitar, I forget about everything on earth but music. Playing a musical instrument helps me relax after a hard day at school or work.

_____

_____

_____

6. Playing basketball teaches you how to work effectively with other people. If you want to win games, you have to learn how to be a team player.

_____

_____

_____

7. My chemistry professor tells us we are stupid if we ask questions about things we don't understand in her lectures. She has no respect for students.

_____

_____

_____

8. My biology professor really wants students to learn. She is willing to stay after class to answer any questions we have about the lecture.

_____

_____

_____

9. Computer games are an expensive hobby. When Nintendo first appeared on the market, it cost $80.00.

_____

_____

_____

10. Car drivers change lanes without giving a warning signal. Driving a car in a city during rush hour makes me a nervous wreck.

_____

_____

_____

## Sentence-Creating Practice

➤ Write eight sentences of your own in which you create your own generalizations and specific examples. Use the connectors *for example* and *for instance*.

1. _____

_____

_____

2. _____

_____

_____

3. _____

_____

_____

4. _____

_____

_____

5. _____

_____

_____

6. _____

_____

_____

7. _____

_____

_____

8. _____

_____

_____

## 6   SENTENCE COMBINING: PUTTING IT TOGETHER

➤ On your own paper, combine the sentences in the groups below. For some, you will be able to use the various sentence connectors you've learned about. For others, you may want to use other connectors. As you are combining the sentences, break this selection into paragraphs and add readers' signposts as you would if you were writing the selection as a composition.

## GOING OUT TO MOVIES VS. RENTING VIDEOTAPES

1. Every Saturday night, my sister and brother-in-law rent a movie on videotape.
2. They want to save money.
3. Videotaped movies are inexpensive.

4. My wife and I want to save money.
5. Sometimes we rent videotaped movies on weekends.
6. Once a month, we go out to a movie.
7. The movie is at a budget theater.

8. We would rather go out to a movie than rent one on videotape.
9. We have three reasons for feeling that way.

10. First of all, going out to a budget theater is almost as inexpensive as renting a videotape.

11. Renting a videotape costs at least $3.50.
12. Budget theaters only charge $1.50 for admission.
13. For only $3.00, two people can see a movie.

14. People live on a limited budget.
15. They can afford to see a movie once a month.

16. People have children.
17. They can afford it.
18. They pay the baby-sitter $5.00.
19. They spend only $8.00 for the evening.

20. They pay $4.50 more than the cost of renting a videotape.
21. They get to go out to a movie.

22. My wife and I think that the $4.50 is money well spent.
23. The atmosphere is so much nicer than it is at home.

24. At the movie, the lights go out.
25. The audience gets quiet.

26. The screen is huge.
27. The picture shows people.
28. The people are larger than in real life.

29. We feel that we are entering a magical world.
30. We feel that we are leaving the real world behind.

31. We rent a videotaped movie.
32. We watch it at home.
33. The room never becomes quiet.
34. Our children keep interrupting us.
35. The telephone rings.

36. We watch the movie on our television.
37. The television has a little screen.
38. The characters are smaller than in real life.

39. We never get to enter a fantasy world.
40. The fantasy world would let us escape from the real world.

41. Finally, my wife and I love our children.
42. We need to get away from them occasionally.

43. We spend so much time with the children.
44. We forget that there was a time.
45. At that time, there were just two people.
46. They were in love.
47. They wanted to get married.

48. We get ready to go out for an evening.
49. We remember those two people.
50. They went on dates.

51. Sometimes we splurge.
52. On the way home, we stop for a piece of pie and a cup of coffee.
53. On the way home, we stop for a tiny pizza and a glass of wine.

54. We pretend that we are teenagers.
55. The teenagers are on a date.
56. We remember why we wanted to get married.

57. In conclusion, going out to see a movie is a little more expensive.
58. My wife and I think that the extra money is worth it.
59. The atmosphere is wonderful.
60. Being alone together is wonderful.

61. Watching a movie at home cannot compete with seeing one at a movie theater.

# 7   USING WHAT YOU HAVE LEARNED IN OTHER WRITING ASSIGNMENTS

Now let's consider ways of applying what you've learned about verbal reasoning to writing problems you may encounter elsewhere.

Any time you are asked to present your opinion on an issue involving a choice, you can ask yourself why you feel the way you do in order to discover if you have good reasons—that is, if you can find generalizations to present to your reader. Then you can search for details that you can use to develop those generalizations into good paragraphs for your essay.

This particular format is quite useful in academic writing tasks. For instance, suppose you are taking an essay examination in a U.S. history course and your professor asks the following question: "Who was the better military leader—Ulysses S. Grant or Robert E. Lee?" Based on what you've learned in the course, you can make your choice and defend it by presenting the reasons and details. Or suppose you are taking a general education course in literature, and you are asked to select two characters from a novel and write a short paper explaining why you would prefer to spend an evening with one of them rather than the other. You could present your choice and defend it by discussing the verbal reasoning that led you to your decision.

You can also use this format in the writing you have to produce on your job. For example, if you, as an assistant manager, are asked to make a recommendation about which of two employees should be promoted, you can present your preference and your reasoning. Or if you, as an accountant, are asked to choose which of two auditing firms your company should hire, you can present your recommendation along with your reasoning. By doing so, you convince your reader to pay attention to your opinion because you've thought seriously about the issue.

Finally, this format is useful any time you want to express your views on a political issue. Suppose the local newspaper has printed an editorial telling your state government that it should not increase the funding it provides to higher education and that instead it should raise tuition costs. If you disagree strongly with the editorial, you can write a letter to the editor presenting your reasons. Or perhaps your local school board has decided to save money by increasing class size, but you think students learn better in small classes. You could write a letter to the school board providing reasons and details to explain your opinion.

## Extra Writing Practice

➤ Select a public issue you feel strongly about, one involving a choice between policies. Write a letter to the editor of the local paper presenting your point of view.

# FIVE

# CLASSIFICATION

## 1 DISCOVERING DETAILS FOR PARAGRAPHS: USING ILLUSTRATIONS

In Chapter 4, you learned how to use two techniques for developing a main idea defending a choice between two subjects: asking the question "Why?" over and over in quest of reasons and details, and using factor analysis as a discovery procedure to aid you in the quest. You can use these same two techniques to develop other kinds of main ideas. In this section, we will employ those techniques to develop a main idea presenting a writer's opinion on *one thing*. We will also consider a technique you can use when you have difficulty finding enough details to create long, well-developed paragraphs.

Consider the following sentences:

I like to play tennis.                 I dislike ironing.

I like my history professor.           I dislike Irma.

Each of these sentences is a potential main idea for a composition in which the writer explains why he or she feels strongly about the particular subject. The writer can turn any of these potential main ideas into the raw material for an essay if he or she can develop reasons to justify the strong feelings. Those reasons can become the topic sentences for paragraphs if the writer can find enough concrete details to develop the paragraphs.

When writers are exploring a topic, sometimes they draw a blank in their attempts to find good specific details. They cannot think of enough details to develop a long paragraph. When this happens to experienced writers, they sometimes come to the conclusion that the particular reason they were seeking to develop is not a good one, and so they reject it. However, at other times they may be convinced that the particular reason is a good one, and so they are determined to include it in the essay. In this instance, they provide an *illustration* or an *anecdote*—that is, a brief story to explain the point they want to make in a paragraph.

To see how this technique works, let's consider the main idea *I like to play tennis.* Suppose a writer who is analyzing the subject of tennis develops the following reasons to explain why this activity is worthwhile:

> Tennis keeps me in good physical condition.
>
> It is good for my emotional health.
>
> It teaches me how to operate successfully in a competitive world.

Then the writer begins to search for details that can be used to develop those reasons into good paragraphs. For the first reason, physical benefits, the writer discovers lots of details:

> The arm I use to swing the racket gets lots of exercise.
>
> When I play tennis, I do lots of running and jumping, so my leg muscles get strong.
>
> When I run and jump, I'm getting aerobic exercise, which is good for my cardiovascular system—my heart and my arteries.
>
> Aerobic exercise is good for my respiratory system—my lungs get a workout when I breathe hard.

Obviously, these details provide the writer with the raw material for a well-developed paragraph.

However, when the writer considers the second reason, benefits for emotional health, the writer can find only one detail:

> Playing tennis makes me relaxed.

Obviously, the writer cannot develop a lengthy paragraph on the basis of this one detail. However, instead of abandoning the reason, the writer can search for a concrete example in his or her experience when playing tennis led to relaxation. For instance, the writer could tell a brief story about a stressful time in his or her life, such as final exam week, and then explain how going to the tennis courts for an hour of hard play helped him or her forget about exams for a little while. As a result, at the end of a tennis match, the writer was relaxed and ready to cope with the tensions of exam week.

Now let's consider the third reason—"It [playing tennis] teaches me how to operate in a competitive world." Suppose that, again, the writer can find few details:

> Tennis teaches me how to behave "with a touch of class" whether I win or lose.
>
> The business world is very competitive.

These two details by themselves would make a very short paragraph. However, if the writer can present an *anecdote*—a little story to illustrate why people will be more effective in the business world if they have learned how to lose gracefully— then the writer can develop a long paragraph. For example, the writer can tell a brief story about a man who worked as a sales representative for a number of corporations, but he could never keep a job. He was a pleasant employee as long as people agreed to buy his product, but when he lost a sale to another company, he would either get depressed or furious. When he was depressed, he would miss work for days, and when he was furious, he would behave obnoxiously toward his co-workers. Eventually, the company he was working for would fire him because he had never learned how to lose gracefully. So playing a competitive game like tennis would teach a person a skill that could be useful on the job.

Writers use two kinds of illustrations or anecdotes. They sometimes tell true stories, and on other occasions they embroider the truth, although the stories could be true. In short, some writers use fictional examples.

## Writing Workshop Exercise

➤ Read the following compositions to answer three questions: (1) What is the main idea of each composition? (2) What reasons does the writer present to justify his or her opinion? (3) Which of the paragraphs are developed using a series of details, and which are developed by presenting an illustration or anecdote?

### COMPOSITION 1: DARTS

I have fallen in love with a game called darts. It is a great pastime that is becoming more popular every day. Why do so many people enjoy throwing little pieces of metal at a cork board with numbers and circles on it? I think that people like to play darts for three reasons.

First of all, people don't have to be in great physical condition in order to play darts. For one thing, throwing darts doesn't demand great physical strength. A 90-pound woman can throw darts just as well as a 200-pound man can. Furthermore, a man who is afraid to lift anything heavier than a glass of beer can certainly lift a dart. For another

thing, throwing darts doesn't force you to engage in strenu-
ous physical activity the way tennis and basketball do. In
darts there is no running or jumping, so people over thirty-
five don't have to get a doctor's permission to play darts. In
fact, people who have heart trouble can play darts. Anyone
with one good arm can become an expert.

A second reason why darts is a popular game is that it is
a social game. Most people are introduced to darts in a bar.
Because they went to the bar to have fun with friends, they
assume that darts is a way to have fun with friends. As a result, although "darters" are competitive about the game,
they do have fun while they're playing. Darts is also social
because of the leisurely pace of the game, which permits
players to talk to one another. While players are waiting for
their turns, they talk to one another about the game. Later,
when the game is over, they sit down at the bar for another
drink, and they continue their conversation about the game.
As a result, they may become friends. So darts is a way of
having fun and meeting new people.

Finally, playing darts provides a way for people to release their anger and frustrations. For instance, suppose you
have had a bad day at work. The customers were obnoxious, and
your boss yelled at you for no reason. Then on your way home,
you were stopped by a cop for going thirty-seven mph in a
thirty-five-mph zone. When you're so angry that you're ready
to scream, you can go to a neighborhood bar and play darts. As
you stare at the dart board, you can pretend that it is your
boss's head or the police officer's head, and you can throw
darts at that imaginary head until you're no longer angry. By
doing so, you'll release your frustrations without losing
your job or ending up in jail.

In conclusion, there are three reasons why darts is a popular game: players don't have to be in great physical condition, players have fun and meet new people while they're playing, and when players need to release their tensions, they can do so on the dart board.

COMPOSITION 2: A TASK I HATE

I enjoy doing most housekeeping chores, but there is one domestic task that I absolutely hate, and that's ironing. I dislike ironing for three reasons.

First of all, ironing is hard on my body. It's very hard on my legs because I can't sit down when I'm ironing and I can't walk around from room to room. Instead, I have to stand for hours in one place, so my legs get tired of standing beside the ironing board. My arms get tired of doing the same thing over and over. My right arm goes back and forth in the same place several times, and I have to press down hard with that arm. My left arm, which just sits on the ironing board holding the fabric, gets tired of staying in the same position. In addition, the heat from the iron makes me extremely uncomfortable. On a cool day, I start to sweat. On a hot day, I get so warm I think I'm going to faint. In short, ironing is a physically unpleasant activity.

Ironing is also a boring activity. My mind has no work to perform when I iron. There is only one way to iron a shirt, only one way to iron a pair of pants, and only one way to iron a skirt. As a result, my mind has nothing interesting to do, so I get very bored. However, I can't let my mind daydream. If I start to daydream, I discover that I have pressed a wrinkle in a shirt or burned my finger. To avoid accidents like these,

I have to concentrate on what I'm doing. What I'm doing is not very interesting. Who can be interested in pushing a hot piece of metal back and forth on a shirt sleeve or a pants leg?

Finally, I hate ironing because it's a job that I should not have to do. I only buy "permanent-press" clothing, so I should never have to iron. Nevertheless, I spend time every week ironing because in the words "permanent-press," "permanent" means a very short time. Let me give you an example to show you what I mean. When I buy a new permanent-press shirt, it looks great the first few times I wash and dry it. But then one Saturday when the shirt's in the dryer, my best friend calls to tell me about the fight she just had with her boyfriend. I can't say, "Sorry, no time to talk. My new shirt's in the dryer." Instead, I comfort my friend, knowing that my shirt will no longer be "permanent press" when I finally remove it from the dryer. Whenever that happens, I feel that the clothing manufacturer cheated me. Therefore, I get angry each time I find myself standing beside an ironing board.

In summary, there are three reasons why I dislike ironing. It's a physically unpleasant activity, it's boring, and it's supposed to be unnecessary. Maybe some day manufacturers will invent fabric that is truly "permanent press." In the meantime, ironing will be my least favorite household chore.

## Journal Assignment

➤ Make a list of people and activities that you like. Then make a list of people and activities that you dislike. When you have finished your lists, examine them carefully. Choose a few items on the lists that you would like to write about. Then use the discovery procedures you've learned about to write a few pages with a main idea like one of the following:

I dislike_____for three reasons.

I like_____for three reasons.

## 2    MAKING A POINT THROUGH CLASSIFICATION

In Chapters 3 and 4 you learned how to develop main ideas for comparison and contrast essays and for essays that defend a choice between two things. In this section we will consider a third kind of main idea: classification.

Although the word *classification* may be unfamiliar to you, you are already acquainted with the concept of classification. In fact, as soon as you started to learn words, you began classifying the people, objects, and activities in your world. You classified people as boys, girls, men, and women; you categorized some objects as food, toys, and furniture; and you classified some activities as walking, running, and dancing.

As you grew older and learned more about the world, you developed yet more categories. For instance, you classified your teachers as good, average, or bad and people as family, friends, acquaintances, or strangers. Later, as you grew interested in particular subjects, you continued your process of classifying the world. If you became interested in cars, you learned to classify them by their manufacturer (Ford, Chevrolet, or Volkswagen) and by the year in which they were made. If you became interested in music, you learned to categorize music as country and western, rock, jazz, heavy metal, or classical.

Since you are already familiar with the concept of classification, now you are ready to learn how to develop main ideas for classification compositions.

Let's begin by looking at the following main ideas, which could be used in classification compositions:

There are *three* kinds of *students at this university:* those who will drop out before they graduate, those who are here just to get a degree, and those who really want an education.

There are *three* kinds of *dangerous drivers:* reckless drivers, self-centered drivers, and supercautious drivers.

There are *four* kinds of *bosses:* the dream boss, the incompetent boss, Mr. Always Right, and Ms. Worry Wart.

There are *three* kinds of *cooks:* terrible cooks, coping cooks, and excellent cooks.

Perhaps the first thing you noticed about these examples is that all of them begin the same way:

There are _____kinds of_____.
                        (number)                                    (subject)

Second, you may have noticed that these sentences contain a punctuation mark that you may not use very often. That punctuation mark (:), which looks like a period on top of another period, is called a *colon*. Colons are often used in written English to tell the reader that a list of things will follow immediately. If you examine the sentences carefully, you will discover that in each one the colon is used to tell the reader that the next thing he or she will see is the list of *kinds* (the list of *classes* or *categories*) the writer is going to discuss in the composition.

Now you need to consider how to discover a classification main idea that you can develop into a composition. Basically, you must do two things. First, you must choose the subject or topic that you think you would like to classify. Second, you have to examine the topic in order to discover how many categories (kinds) you want to discuss.

For instance, suppose you want to write an essay on kinds of friends. As you think about friends you've had in your life, you might decide that you want to discuss four different categories: best friends, casual acquaintances, friends to go out with, and two-faced friends. Or perhaps you might decide to write about kinds of drivers. As you explored the subject, you might classify three kinds of drivers: excellent drivers, average drivers, and terrible drivers.

Suppose, however, that you think you would like to write an essay on the kinds of "car-owners" you have met, but you have difficulty coming up with specific categories. If that happens, you can try using factor analysis as a discovery procedure. For example, you could try to develop categories of car-owners based on economic considerations. By doing so, you might discover you could write about three kinds of car-owners: budget-car people, expensive-car people, and middle-price-car people. Or you could investigate the possibility of classifying car-owners "emotionally," that is, by how they feel toward their vehicles. You might come up with a classification of car-owners with categories like the following: those who see a car as "just transportation," those who think of a car as a trusted companion, and those who are madly in love with their cars. For still another example, you could explore potential categories of car-owners based on the physical characteristics of the cars they buy: sports-car owners, luxury-car owners, and family-car owners.

## Journal Assignment

➤ Choose some topics that you think could be developed into classification compositions. Develop classification main ideas for several of those topics.

If you have difficulty thinking of subjects, you might consider some of the following:

| | | |
|---|---|---|
| bosses | teachers | students |
| dates | bus drivers | bus passengers |
| cardplayers | roommates | parents |

## 3    CONSIDERING THE READER'S NEEDS: AVOIDING IRRELEVANT DETAILS

In Chapter 3, we considered the reader's problem of trying to understand the "point," the main idea the writer is trying to communicate. In this section, we will examine the implications of that problem for a classification main idea.

As you know, different people classify the world in different ways. Some people see only two kinds of cars: expensive and inexpensive. Others know so much about automobiles that they have a long list of categories including such information as manufacturer, year, and model. For some people a football player is a football player, but others know the difference between running backs, tight ends, and wide receivers.

Obviously, if different people classify the world in distinct ways, you cannot assume that your reader will be familiar with your particular categories. To make sure that the reader will understand your classification, you will need to provide concrete details, perhaps through examples or illustrations that will give your reader all the information he or she needs in order to understand what you are trying to say. As to how much information is necessary, at this point in your development as a writer, you should assume that your reader is intelligent but doesn't really know much about your world. Therefore, you need to give the reader a great deal of information.

The one kind of information you should *not* give your reader is *irrelevant* information. Such information may be true, but it is not very useful for the reader who is trying to understand your ideas. For instance, suppose you're writing a composition about kinds of car-owners based on the emotions they feel toward their cars, and you think of your Uncle Henry as an example of a person who considers his car "just transportation." You decide to describe his car, which clearly shows how Uncle Henry feels about cars. You explain that the car, which is eight years old, has a lot of rust damage on the body, but your uncle won't get it repainted because he doesn't care what it looks like. Since all he cares about is that it still runs perfectly, he refuses to spend money to improve its appearance. Your readers will find these details both useful and *relevant* for helping them understand your classification. However, if you also mention that Uncle Henry is really a nice man who gave you a chess set on your birthday, your reader will consider that information *irrelevant* to your main idea because it has nothing to do with Uncle Henry's feelings about his car. This brings us to our ninth guideline for good writing:

> *Guideline 9:* Good writing does not include irrelevant information.

Sometimes it is not easy to recognize the difference between relevant and useful information that helps the reader understand your ideas, and irrelevant, useless information that is of no use to the reader. For instance, if you are writing about Uncle Henry's car, and you tell the reader that his car is so ugly you refuse to ride in it, then your reader will understand that you hate the car but won't know why you feel this way. On the other hand, if you give relevant details about the car, then the reader will understand your point of view.

In conclusion, when you are writing, keep your reader in mind, and make sure that your information is relevant and will be useful to the reader.

## Writing Workshop Exercise

➤ Read the following compositions with these questions in mind: (1) What is the main idea of the essays? (2) How well does each essay provide details relevant to the main idea?

### COMPOSITION 1: THREE KINDS OF COOKS

I love to eat, so I appreciate good cooking. Unfortunately, when I am invited to dinner at someone else's home, I cannot assume that I am going to enjoy the meal because not all cooks are good cooks. In fact, my experience has taught me that there are three kinds of cooks: the terrible cooks, the coping cooks, and the good cooks.

First, let's consider terrible cooks. They plan fancy menus, but the food never tastes as good as it sounds. My Aunt Betty's meals are like that. Whenever we're invited to her house, I try to find some excuse that will convince my parents that I really cannot go to Aunt Betty's. Sometimes, I've even decided to stay home and study because I know how terrible the food will taste. Sometimes, when my parents insist that I

go. I put some antacid tablets in my pocket and try to prepare
myself for the horrible food. The worst part of it all is the
moment when I have to lie and say that I really loved the
food.

The second kind of cook is the coping cook. The food
isn't great, but it's edible, so you know you won't get indigestion. My sister Helen's meals are like that. She's only
been married a year, and she had never cooked a meal before
she got married. So she depends on prepared foods, but the
food is okay. As a result, I enjoy going to her house for dinner.

The last kind of cook is the good cook. My cousin Bill is
an example of this kind of cook. The food is just fantastic.
In fact, his meals are so good that I've considered breaking
a date in order to accept an invitation to his house. He makes
superb paella that is so good that I always eat several help-
ings. Moreover, his cakes and pies are out of this world.
When I tell Bill a meal was great, I really mean it.

Now that we've considered the three kinds of cooks, we
only need to do one more thing. We need to learn how to recognize a good cook before we are invited to dinner. Unfortunately, I haven't learned how to do that.


COMPOSITION 2: THREE KINDS OF COOKS


I love to eat, so I appreciate good cooking. Unfortunately, when I am invited to dinner at someone else's home, I
cannot assume that I am going to enjoy the meal because not
all cooks are good cooks. In fact, my experience has taught
me that there are three kinds of cooks: the terrible cooks,
the coping cooks, and the good cooks.

First, let's consider terrible cooks. My Aunt Betty is an example of a terrible cook. She plans fancy menus that sound wonderful. For instance, a dinner might include sweet and sour pork, stuffed baked potatoes, green beans with mushroom sauce, hot rolls, and a tossed salad with vinegar and oil dressing. However, the food never tastes as good as it sounds. The pork is so sweet that it reminds you of candy. The potatoes have been cooked too long, so they taste like powder. The green beans, which have been boiled for hours, have no taste at all; in addition, the mushroom sauce has lumps of raw flour. The hot rolls are like pieces of lead that fall to the bottom of your stomach and lie there. The salad dressing, which seems to contain only vinegar, brings tears to your eyes. By the end of the meal, you wish you had brought along some antacid tablets for the indigestion you know you're going to get.

The second kind of cook is the coping cook. Coping cooks are people like my sister Helen, who has learned to let other people do the cooking. She may plan a menu similar to the one the terrible cook prepared, but the food will be edible because she depends on experts. Helen serves sweet and sour pork that she bought at the local Chinese restaurant. Her stuffed baked potatoes and her green beans were bought in the frozen food section at the supermarket, and the mushroom sauce was made from a mix. The hot rolls come from the local bakery, and the salad dressing comes from a bottle. Although the food may not be spectacularly good, you don't get indigestion.

Finally, there are the good cooks who know how to perform miracles in the kitchen. My cousin Bill is an example of a fantastic cook. When he prepares a fancy menu, the food always tastes better than it sounds. The sauce on the sweet and sour pork is a delightful mixture of sweet and sour tastes. The stuffed baked potatoes are crisp on top and moist on the inside, so they melt in your mouth. The green beans are crunchy and flavorful, and the homemade mushroom sauce is rich and creamy. The hot rolls, which were made from scratch, are so light that they almost float off the plate. The salad dressing is the cook's creation. The vinegar and oil are in perfect balance, and there is a slight touch of garlic along with some strange herbs that add a marvelous flavor to the salad. In short, when you tell a cook like Bill that the meal was superb, you mean it.

Now that we've considered the three kinds of cooks, we only need to do one more thing. We need to learn how to recognize a good cook before we are invited for dinner. Unfortunately, I haven't learned how to do that.

## 4   MORE ON READERS' SIGNPOSTS

In Chapter 3 you learned that good writers provide *readers' signposts* to help the reader follow the ideas in the composition. In that chapter, you learned about three kinds of signposts: main ideas, topic sentences for paragraphs, and phrases that signal a conclusion. In this section, we will consider another kind of signpost—what some textbooks call *transitional expressions*.

Transitional expressions are certain words or phrases that you can use in the middle of a composition to help the reader keep track of where he or she is in the essay at any given moment. These words or phrases include words like the following:

| | | | |
|---|---|---|---|
| first | next | on the other hand | as a result |
| second | for example | moreover | therefore |
| third | for instance | in addition | consequently |
| finally | however | also | |
| then | nevertheless | furthermore | |

(As you have probably noticed from this list, many of these words and phrases can also be used as sentence connectors.)

In order to see these transitional words in use, reread the compositions titled "Darts" and "A Task I Hate" in Section 1, and the compositions titled "Three Kinds of Cooks" in Section 3. As you do so, underline all the readers' signposts you can find, including not only transitional expressions but also the main ideas, topic sentences for paragraphs, and any conclusion signals. When you're finished, you will be ready to practice adding readers' signposts as you do the following writing workshop exercise in order to learn how to use them in your own writing.

## Writing Workshop Exercise

➤ Read the following composition. Then rewrite it by adding readers' signposts, including transitional expressions.

### THREE KINDS OF DANGEROUS DRIVERS

I've been driving a car for almost ten years. During those years, I've learned to recognize three kinds of drivers who should not be allowed on the road: self-centered drivers, supercautious drivers, and reckless drivers.

Self-centered drivers assume that they own the road. My sister Helen is like that. She wants to go to a store, but she can't find a parking place close enough to suit her. She will double-park, leave the car, and do her shopping. She's driving along, and she's in a hurry. If the stoplight up ahead turns yellow, she'll speed up and go through the intersection after the light turns red. She's driving someplace, and she's ahead of time. If the stoplight turns yellow as she reaches it, she'll slam on her brakes because she has plenty of time. She just assumes that the drivers behind her will be able to stop on a dime. If she's in the lefthand lane and she suddenly needs to turn right, she'll turn right across two lanes of traffic without looking to see if any cars are coming.

Supercautious drivers are terrified of having an accident. My Uncle Elmer is like that. He's sure his brakes will fail if a car pulls in front of him. He only drives twenty miles an hour in a 30-mile-per-hour zone. When he stops at a stop sign, he won't drive across the street if he sees a car within a block of the intersection. Sometimes it takes five minutes before he gets brave enough to enter the intersection. If he thinks a stoplight is about to turn yellow, he slows down so that he won't have to stop quickly. If there's a car in front of him, he'll slow down to leave four or five carlengths between his car and the one ahead of him. I'm scared to death to ride with him. Other drivers get so angry that they take chances in order to get around him.

Everyone knows about reckless drivers. My cousin Bart is a reckless driver. He always drives at least ten miles an hour faster than the speed limit, and sometimes he drives twenty miles an hour faster. If a stoplight turns yellow, he steps on the gas even if he knows that the light will turn red before he gets to the intersection. If he's in the lefthand lane and he thinks the righthand lane is moving faster, he'll cut in front of a car in order to get in the faster lane. If he sees a curve in the road ahead, he never slows down before he enters the curve. If the car starts to skid, he thinks it's exciting. He always tailgates any driver who dares to get ahead of him. It never occurs to him that the driver in front might suddenly slam on the brakes.

There are three kinds of dangerous drivers: those who assume there are no other cars on the road, those who drive so cautiously they infuriate other drivers, and those who take chances with their own lives as well as the lives of their passengers.

## COMPOSITION ASSIGNMENT

Choose one of the classification main ideas that you developed in the journal assignment at the end of Section 2 and develop it into a composition. Be sure to provide relevant details, perhaps through illustrations or anecdotes, so that your reader can understand your way of classifying your topic. Also, be sure to provide signposts for your reader and to proofread your composition carefully before turning it in.

## 5    SENTENCE COMBINING IN WRITTEN ENGLISH: APPOSITIVE CONSTRUCTIONS

When you talk, no one expects you to express your ideas precisely, using the fewest possible words. The listener understands that you are thinking as you talk, so he or she cannot expect you to worry about how you express your ideas. But when you write, the reader assumes that you have the time to stop and think about how you are going to express your ideas. Therefore, the reader expects you to express your ideas precisely.

As you have already learned, the reader also expects you to provide lots of details in order to make sure that he or she understands what you are trying to say. At this point, you may be thinking that you are expected to do two contradictory things when you write: to use the fewest possible words, but to provide lots of information. Although the two may seem to be contradictory, they really are not. It is possible to write precisely *and* at the same time provide a great deal of information.

How can you accomplish this goal? As you develop your writing skills, you will discover a number of sentence patterns that writers use to add details as economically as possible. In this section, we will consider a pattern that uses what is called an *appositive construction*. In order to discover how this construction works, let's begin by considering the following groups of sentences:

I once gave a ride to Artur Rubinstein. He was a famous pianist.
My grandmother grew up in Allenville. It is a small town in
    southeast Missouri.

As you know from Chapter 1, you could combine these sentences using relative pronouns, as the following sentences illustrate:

I once gave a ride to Artur Rubinstein, who was a famous pianist.
My grandmother grew up in Allenville, which is a small town in
    southeast Missouri.

It's also possible to combine these sentences more economically by using appositive constructions, as in the following sentences:

> I once gave a ride to Artur Rubinstein, a famous pianist.
> My grandmother grew up in Allenville, a small town in southeast Missouri.

As you can guess from the above examples, an appositive is a phrase (a group of words) that you can add to a sentence in order to give the reader more information about a person or place that you are writing about. Also, as the above examples show, when you add an appositive to a sentence, you need to set off the appositive with a comma. See the following examples:

> My uncle is a podiatrist. A podiatrist is a foot doctor.
> Melissa is majoring in zoology. Zoology is the study of animals.

When these pairs of sentences are combined, the following sentences result:

> My uncle is a podiatrist, a foot doctor.
> Melissa is majoring in zoology, the study of animals.

The appositives we have considered so far come at the end of a sentence, but they may appear elsewhere in a sentence. The following pairs of sentences require this pattern:

> My sister refused to go out on strike. She is a Kansas City fire fighter.
> Mr. Gonzalez is the lawyer for you. He is an expert on consumer protection.

These pairs of sentences can be combined as follows:

> My sister, a Kansas City fire fighter, refused to go out on strike.
> Mr. Gonzalez, an expert on consumer protection, is the lawyer for you.

In these examples, you will notice that when an appositive is placed in the middle of a sentence, two commas are needed to set off the appositive.

## Sentence-Combining Practice

➤ Combine the following pairs of sentences using appositive constructions.

1. I just finished reading *Bury My Heart at Wounded Knee*. It is a history of Native Americans.

_____

_____

2. Stephanie wants to major in geology. Geology is the study of the earth's crust.

_____

_____

3. Wallace Stevens was an insurance salesman. He was a great twentieth-century poet.

_____

_____

4. Amy Tan will give a talk on Thursday. She is an important Chinese-American writer.

_____

_____

5. Paulette's father will be interviewed on TV tonight. He is a Chicago alderman.

_____

_____

6. Max comes from San Lorenzo. It is a small village in Puerto Rico.

_____

_____

7. George Eliot was a woman. She was a major British novelist of the nineteenth century.

_____

_____

8. Russ really enjoyed *My Brilliant Career*. It was a movie about an independent woman.

_____

_____

9. Millie once met Ralph Ellison. He was a famous African-American writer.

_____

_____

10. Keith hates linguistics. Linguistics is the study of language.

_____

_____

## Sentence-Creating Exercise

➤ Create ten sentences of your own in which you use appositives to give the reader information in an economical way.

1. _____

_____

2. _____

_____

3. _____

_____

4. _____

_____

5. _____

_____

6. _____

_____

7. _____

_____

8. _____

_____

9. _____

_____

10. _____

_____

## 6   SENTENCE COMBINING: PUTTING IT TOGETHER

➤ On your own paper, combine the sentences in the groups below, using the sentence connectors you've learned about up to this point. As you are combining the sentences, break the selection into paragraphs and add readers' signposts as you would if you were writing it as a composition.

### THREE KINDS OF NEIGHBORS

1. I have lived in many apartment buildings.
2. I have had many neighbors.

3. From my experiences, I have concluded that there are three kinds of neighbors.
4. One kind is the neighbor from hell.
5. One kind is the mystery neighbor.
6. One kind is the good neighbor.

7. Neighbors from hell are the worst kind of neighbor you can have.
8. They make your life a constant nightmare.

9. The Hills are examples of bad neighbors.
10. The Hills are the family who live in the apartment above mine.

11. The Hills have no consideration for other tenants.
12. They are extremely noisy.
13. They yell and scream at each other for hours on end.

14. They finally stop screaming.
15. You think that you can get some rest.
16. Then they play loud music until 4:00 in the morning.

17. You are afraid to complain about the noise.
18. They will probably decide to get revenge.
19. They will start pounding on the floor.
20. They will ring your doorbell in the middle of the night.

21. The mystery neighbor is the invisible person.
22. You almost never see or hear that person.

23. The Jacksons are examples of mystery neighbors.
24. The Jacksons are the family in the apartment next door to mine.

25. I saw their name on the mailbox.
26. I know their name is Jackson.
27. I'm not sure what they look like.

28. They seem to be very considerate of other tenants.
29. I have never heard them make any noise.

30. Sometimes I wonder whether anybody actually lives in that apartment.
31. I see magazines addressed to them in the recycling bin.
32. I know someone lives there.

33. They don't cause any trouble.
34. They don't keep me up at night.

35. They also never do anything for me.
36. I would never consider asking them for a favor.
37. They wouldn't know who I am.

38. Good neighbors make your life a joy.
39. They don't bother you.
40. They are on hand when you need them.

41. Mr. Ortega is an example of a good neighbor.
42. Mr. Ortega was the elderly man who lived next door to me in my last building.

43. He never made any noise.
44. He almost never complained about my own noise.

45. He was very friendly.
46. He spoke each time he saw me.
47. He asked about my family.

48. He was very helpful.
49. I needed a stick of butter.
50. I could ask him for it.
51. I saw him in the hall taking down his garbage.
52. He offered to take mine as well.

53. Mystery neighbors are better than bad neighbors.
54. Good neighbors are a treasure.
55. We all appreciate such a treasure.

## 7    USING WHAT YOU HAVE LEARNED IN OTHER WRITING ASSIGNMENTS

In this section, we will explore ways of applying what you've learned in this chapter to writing assignments that you are given in the world outside the English classroom.

In most of the courses you take in college, you will be introduced to classification in one form or another. In biology, you will learn about kinds of plant and animal life; in political science, you will learn about different kinds of political systems; and in anthropology, you will learn about types of human cultures. From this discussion, you can guess that any time you hear words such as *kinds* or *types,* you have encountered ideas that can be developed into compositions or papers that will permit you to use what you've learned about classification.

Classification will be useful to you not only while you're in school, but also in the world outside. Almost any job that you might consider will at some point deal with kinds, types, or categories. In a supermarket, for example, you must deal with different kinds of food products: dairy products, meat, produce (fruits and vegetables), bakery goods, pet foods, canned foods, frozen foods, and so on. An employee in a discount store must work with departments that display different kinds of merchandise: clothing, cosmetics, furniture, kitchen utensils, small appliances. A criminal lawyer has to consider different kinds of crime, and a teacher must work with different types of students.

So classification will be useful to you in the world of work. For example, your boss might ask you to write a report on different kinds of computers that your company might buy, and you could use classification as a way of organizing your ideas. Or your boss might ask you to write a report about how well different kinds of cameras are selling. Again, classification would be useful.

In summary, certain words—*kinds, types,* and *categories*—usually indicate that classification will be a useful way of developing your ideas.

## Extra Writing Practice

➤ Think about the subjects you are taking in school. Have any of your professors used classification as a way of organizing their lectures? Think about your job. Is classification ever used where you work? Make a list of different classifications that you can think of. Then choose one subject, and write a classification composition on that topic.

# SIX

# EXPLORING COMPLEX ISSUES

## 1  MORE ABOUT PARAGRAPHS: WRITING SUMMARIES

In Chapters 2 through 5, you were taught several things about paragraphs. First you learned the definition of a paragraph as a section of a composition that deals with a particular point. Next, you learned that writers sometimes use topic sentences to introduce the new points that will be discussed in particular paragraphs—points that they develop by providing details. Finally, you learned that writers can use illustrations or anecdotes to develop paragraphs.

In this section, we will make use of your knowledge of paragraphing as we consider two problems you face when you write papers in your academic courses: (1) You must make decisions about when to start new paragraphs. (2) You must write effective summaries of material that you read as you research particular topics.

In order to help you solve the first problem, we will begin by considering what you have learned about paragraphing for a comparison and contrast essay. As you remember, in Chapter 3 you were told that comparison and contrast essays can easily be divided into four paragraphs: an introductory paragraph, a paragraph on similarities, a paragraph on differences, and a concluding paragraph. However, if you reread the essay titled "Myself Then and Now" in Chapter 4, Section 1 (page 61), you will discover that it is divided into seven paragraphs. If you examine that essay carefully, you will easily discover why it was divided into more than four paragraphs.

Let's assume the writer of "Myself Then and Now" had planned a four-paragraph composition. However, as she was writing, she kept finding more details to use in the paragraphs on differences and similarities. She found so many details that her paragraphs became longer and longer. Finally, she concluded that the paragraphs had become too long and that they needed to be divided into shorter paragraphs. To use our analogy with bees from Chapter 2, the writer decided that the beehive of ideas in each paragraph had become so crowded that it was time to divide those two long paragraphs into shorter ones.

When the writer decided to break those long paragraphs into shorter ones, she searched for logical places to make the breaks. For instance, she split the paragraph on differences when she came to the end of her discussion of how her physical appearance had changed. She split it again when she finished her discussion of how her behavior had changed.

At this point, you should be developing an understanding of how writers decide when to start a new paragraph. Now let's consider the issue from a different perspective. Examine the following paragraph, which is a summary of one of the compositions that you read in Chapter 4, Section 2 (p. 64):

```
      Dogs make better pets than cats for three reasons. First
of all, dogs are much more intelligent than cats. For exam-
ple, dogs can be taught to perform tricks, but cats cannot.
Second, because dogs are so intelligent, they are much more
helpful to their owners than cats are. For instance, dogs can
fetch your slippers and bark to scare away robbers, but cats
can't do anything except lie around and look pretty. Finally,
dogs are much more affectionate companions than cats are.
Dogs will go walking with you, and they will let you pet them
whenever you want to. Cats only show affection when they feel
like it. In short, people who want a smart, useful, affec-
tionate pet will be much happier with a dog than they will be
with a cat.
```

This paragraph develops one point: that there are three reasons for preferring dogs over cats.

If you take a few minutes to reread the composition about dogs and cats, you will understand more about how our discussion of bees back in Chapter 2 relates to the question of when a writer decides that he or she has reached a new point and should, therefore, begin a new paragraph. In the original composition, the writer provided many details to give the reader more information about why dogs make better pets than cats. As a result, the composition became so long that the writer divided it into five paragraphs.

As you compare the paragraph and the whole composition, you will also receive useful clues about how to write summaries of long passages that you read when you research topics for your academic courses. When writing the summary, the writer removed most of the details. As a result, the ideas in the composition shrank until they could fit in one paragraph.

For another example of a summary, consider the following paragraph, which condenses Composition 2 from Chapter 5, Section 3 (page 90):

```
     There are three kinds of cooks. One kind is the terrible
cook, who uses fancy recipes, but doesn't realize that he or
she fails to produce edible food. The second kind is the cop-
ing cook, who knows that he or she is not a good cook and,
therefore, lets the experts do the cooking. The final kind of
cook is the fantastic cook, who uses exotic recipes and pro-
duces meals that are so good you want to go on eating forever.
```

This summary paragraph develops one point: that there are three kinds of cooks.

A rereading of the original composition shows how the writer of this paragraph removed most of the details in order to present a brief summary of the main points from the original composition. Similarly, in your academic courses, in your summaries of the material you've read you will be expected to eliminate the details that writers provide to help the reader understand the ideas.

## Journal Assignment

➤ Write a one-paragraph summary of Composition 2 in Chapter 4, Section 2 (page 66). Then write one-paragraph summaries of the two compositions in Chapter 5, Section 1 (pages 82 and 84). Finally, write a one-paragraph summary of the classification essay you wrote in Chapter 5.

## 2   CONSIDERING COMPLEX ISSUES: ADVANTAGES AND DISADVANTAGES

In Chapter 4, you read two different compositions on cats versus dogs. One explained why cats make better pets, while the other explained why dogs make better pets. When you were reading those essays, you may have concluded that each writer was probably guilty of oversimplifying the situation. After all, you may have thought, there surely must be times when "dog-lovers" hate to go out to walk their dogs, especially on cold, rainy days, and there must be times when "cat-lovers" feel so sad or lonesome they wish that their cats would show the kind of devoted affection that dogs provide.

You may have concluded that each writer was being just a little dishonest by ignoring the imperfections of his or her pet; certainly, each animal has its advantages and its disadvantages. When you formed that conclusion, you may have wondered whether writers ever choose to be completely honest and admit that the situation they're discussing is actually somewhat complicated. You may also have wondered whether there are techniques writers can use when they want to discuss such complex issues. In this section, we will consider one of those techniques—specifically, an organization pattern that is called *advantages and disadvantages*.

You're already familiar with reasoning by advantage and disadvantage. In fact, you use it any time you decide whether you should eat an extra piece of cake or pie. You consider the advantage—the wonderful taste—and you weigh the disadvantage—the extra calories. Then you decide if the good sensation in your mouth will be so pleasant that you're willing to suffer the bad consequences. For another example, if you are trying to decide whether to work fewer hours at your part-time job, you consider the disadvantage—you will earn less money. Next you weigh the advantage—you will have more time to study. Then you finally decide which is more important, the loss of some money or the extra time to study. In other words, you decide whether the disadvantage outweighs the advantage, or vice versa.

Now we need to consider how you can use what you know about advantage-and-disadvantage reasoning in your writing. To do so, let's return to the essay you wrote in Chapter 4 defending a choice between two things. Suppose you wanted to write an essay explaining why you like to play football better than you like soccer, and you were using factor analysis to search for reasons. When you thought about *physical reasons*, you may have realized that football has a major disadvantage. You run a greater risk of serious injury when you play football. That disadvantage was actually a good reason to prefer soccer, but you didn't use that reason, because it was irrelevant to your main idea, which stated that football is a better sport. However, if you had been writing an advantage-and-disadvantage essay, you could have written a paragraph in which you admitted that soccer does have one major advantage over football: namely, less risk of serious injury. Then you could have explained that, nevertheless, you still like football better than soccer for a few reasons, which you would discuss in the next paragraphs.

For another example, let's consider the essay you wrote in Chapter 5, Section 1, explaining why you liked or disliked something. Suppose you were writing about why you like your part-time job in a day-care center. As you used factor analysis you explored economic issues and recognized that your job has a major disadvantage: You don't earn much money. However, you didn't present that issue because it was irrelevant to your main idea—why you like your job. On the other hand, if you had been writing an advantage-and-disadvantage paper, you could have written a paragraph on the major disadvantage, the salary. Next, you could have explained that you like the job anyway because it has several advantages. You would then have presented those advantages in several paragraphs.

To summarize what you've learned, when you write an advantage-and-disadvantage composition, you can use a main idea like one of the following:

> While the game of football has one major disadvantage when compared to soccer, I prefer football for several reasons.
>
> While my job at a daycare center has one major drawback, I still like it because it has several advantages.

With main ideas like these, you can write essays in which you explain why you like something, even though you know there are reasons for holding the opposite point of view.

But perhaps you want to explain why you dislike something, even though you recognize there are a few good reasons for liking it. Then you can use a main idea like one of the following:

> While the game of soccer has a few advantages, I dislike it for several reasons.
>
> While my job as a bus driver has a few advantages, I dislike it because it has several disadvantages.

With main ideas like these, writers can make it clear to the reader that they know the issue is complicated.

Now you are ready to see what such an essay looks like when it is fully developed.

## Writing Workshop Exercise

➤ Read the essay below to answer these questions: (1) What generalization does the writer present as the major disadvantage of the single life? (2) What generalizations does the writer present as the advantages of the single life? (3) Do you think the writer has good reasons for feeling the way he does?

### THE SINGLE LIFE

Like most people, I've spent a great deal of time observing married people and single people. Also, like most adults, I have been married myself as well as single. Based on what I've seen and experienced, if I had my life to live over again, I would wait longer before I married. Even though the single life has a few disadvantages, there are some very real advantages in being single.

Let me begin by admitting that the single life is not the perfect life. Being single has one major disadvantage; namely, there are times when single people are very much alone. For instance, if they've had a bad day at school or work, they want someone to share their troubles with when they get home. Married people have someone who will be there when they get home, but single people go home to empty apartments with no one there to provide comfort or warmth. Even worse for single people are the times when they get sick. On those occasions, they have no one in the house to go to the druggist for a prescription, to go to the supermarket if the refrigerator is empty, or to drive you to the doctor's office or the hospital. As a result, being single occasionally means feeling very much alone.

Yet there are definite advantages in being single. First of all, single people have freedom of movement. They can go where they want to go when they want to. When I was single, if there was a movie I really wanted to see, I would call my friends until I found one who wanted to see the movie; as a result, I never missed a movie I wanted to see. However, now that I am married, whenever there is a movie I want to see, I have to convince my wife to go see it; as a result, I miss a lot of movies. Not only do I find that I can't do some things I want to do, but I also find that I have to do things I don't want to do. I have to watch the opera or ballet performances on television in order to get my wife to watch the football games I want to see. I have to go to plays with my wife in order to get her to go to baseball games with me.

As another advantage, single people have financial independence. They can spend money when they want to. A single man who has the money for a new car can pick it out and buy it. A married man has to discuss the matter with his wife and convince her that they need a new car and that the car he wants is the best one available to meet their needs. A single woman who wants a new coat can buy one when she feels like it, without worrying about whether her husband will think that she has paid too much money for a coat that she doesn't really need. Finally, no single person ever bought a brown rug because the wife wanted a blue rug and the husband wanted a green one, so they settled for a color that neither one really wanted but both could live with.

In conclusion, being single has its disadvantages; however, there are some definite advantages. If I had my life to live over, I would have waited until I was thirty before I got married. Then I would have had plenty of time to enjoy the pleasures of the single life before I settled down.

## Journal Assignment

➤ Choose some subjects that are complex—that have both good and bad characteristics. Do some prewriting to explore the advantages and disadvantages and to discover whether you can find some generalizations and concrete details that you could use to develop an advantage-and-disadvantage essay. If you have difficulty finding possible topics, you might consider one of the following:

| | |
|---|---|
| high heels | being married |
| sports cars | taking public transportation |
| owning a pet | your house or apartment |
| owning a car | counting calories |
| smoking cigarettes | eating low-cholesterol food |
| fast food restaurants | |

## 3    THINKING ABOUT THE READER: ADMITTING DIFFERENT POINTS OF VIEW

In Chapter 4, we discussed one problem that you as a writer will face whenever you're defending an opinion on a topic. Specifically, we considered the fact that you cannot assume that your readers share your opinion. We also examined one technique you can use in order to try to get your readers to respect your ideas even if they disagree with you—the technique of presenting good reasons with lots of supporting details. In this section, we'll consider another technique you can use in the hope of convincing the reader that your point of view should be respected. With this particular technique, the writer not only admits that the topic is complicated, but also demonstrates that he or she is fully aware of the complications.

As you might expect, writers sometimes want to make it clear that they appreciate the complexity of an issue, particularly when they fear that the reader may hold a strongly opposed point of view. To understand why writers are especially concerned about such readers, let's return to the subject of the essays on "Cats vs. Dogs" in Chapter 5. As we discussed in the last section, when you read those essays, you may have concluded that the writers were being a little dishonest by refusing to admit that their pets were not perfect. When you formed that conclusion, you may have felt a little bothered that the writers were oversimplifying the issues. But you didn't get really upset because they were expressing their opinions on a relatively minor issue—pets.

You might have become more upset, however, if the writers had been addressing major issues, such as whether abortion should be legal or whether the death penalty should be abolished. You might not be willing to forgive writers who oversimplify such important topics. You might be especially upset if you believe you have good reasons for disagreeing with the writer's opinion.

On the other hand, if the writer admits that the opposite perspective has some validity and then presents some of the reasons for holding this point of view, the reader may be forced to admit that perhaps the writer really has given serious attention to the issue. As a result, the reader will be less likely to become very upset with the writer. In short, by recognizing the possible arguments of people who hold a different opinion, writers can make their opponents more willing to respect the writers' perspectives.

Thus we can summarize our tenth guideline for good writing:

> *Guideline 10:* Good writers know that if they make it clear that they recognize the complexity of the subject, they are more likely to gain the respect of a reader who holds the opposite point of view.

To see this rule in operation, we will now perform a writing workshop exercise.

## Writing Workshop Exercise

➤ Read the following composition. Point out the places where the writer tries to convince the reader that she is aware of the complexity of the topic, and describe how she does this.

EXERCISE

Every New Year's Day, I make a resolution that in the coming year, I will definitely go to the YMCA in my neighborhood at least three times a week in order to get regular exercise. On January 2, I go to the "Y" to buy a membership and then head for the locker room to don my "sweats" or my swimsuit as I begin my annual battle against the bulges in my body.

Before I know it, it's the end of March, and I suddenly realize that it's been weeks since I went near the Y. I feel overwhelmed with guilt. I promise myself that I'll go to the Y for sure the next day or the day after. But something extremely important comes up, preventing me from exercising the next day or the next. Soon I'm forced to admit that once again I've failed to keep my New Year's resolution to get regular exercise. Why do I go through this same routine year after year? It's simple. I know that exercise is good for me, but I hate it.

In my heart of hearts, I know that if I get regular aerobic exercise, I will probably live longer than I will if I don't exercise. I've read all the articles on maintaining good health that tell me that my cardiovascular system will love me if I swim 25 laps, three times a week. Or if I don't like swimming, jogging is an excellent way to get my heart pumping to build up its strength while my lungs inhale and exhale, increasing their capacity. There's also the stationary bike, on which I can pedal away, as I give my heart and lungs a good workout. If I do any of those activities regularly, my body will become so healthy that I'll probably be fit as a fiddle until I'm in my eighties.

Also, I know that if I get regular exercise, I will look better. I'll burn off so many calories that the pounds on my body will melt away without my having to think about going on a diet. Not only will I become slender, but my muscle tone will be phenomenal. My thighs and my buttocks will be solid instead of flabby. My tummy will be absolutely flat, and my upper arms will be like rocks. Finally, my torso will look terrific. I've seen how terrific Cher looks, even though she's over 45. She swears she owes it all to regular exercise, and I believe her. I'm sure I too will have a wonderful bod at 45 if I just follow her advice and make time in my schedule every week for exercise.

However, even though I know how good exercise is for me, I always quit it because I hate to exercise. For one thing, I really don't like to sweat. No matter how great my hair looks when I go to the Y, I know the sweaty strands will be falling in my eyes after 15 minutes of jogging, unless I want to use a sweatband, which will totally destroy my hairdo. No matter how perfect my makeup is, as soon as I get on that stationary bike, my pores will start expanding to let all that moisture out of my body, and drip goes the makeup. Worse still, when I sweat, my face gets bright red and stays bright red for an

hour after I quit exercising. In fact, I look so terrible
when I sweat I've had doctors ask me if I've had my blood
pressure checked recently. Needless to say, I know better
than to think I'll meet the man of my dreams when I'm pumping
iron at the local YMCA.

For people who hate to sweat, the preferred alternative
is swimming laps, an activity which is, to put it mildly,
boring. I travel from one end of the pool to the other, putting my face in the water, then turning it to the side to
breathe, then putting my face in the water before turning it
to the side to breathe, etc., etc., etc. When I reach the end
of the pool, I get to turn around and follow the same routine
until I get back where I started. Then I must turn around
once again, and so on until I've swum my 25 laps. It's possible, of course, to vary the stroke: I can back-stroke one
lap, then do the crawl, then switch to the breast-stroke,
and finally the side-stroke. Then it's time to go back to
the back-stroke, etc., etc., etc. What could be more
boring?

For people who hate to sweat and hate to swim, what's
left? As any physical fitness freak will tell you, there's always walking. How right they are! There's always walking, an
activity that can be especially pleasant on a sunny day, when
the weather's not too hot and not too cold, unless I encounter a person who desires my company when I have no interest in
that person's company. Or maybe I'll encounter a less than
friendly dog, or perhaps I'll step in something that some dog
deposited. So even when the weather's perfect, walking has
its perils. When the weather isn't perfect, I get soaking wet
unless I want to go to the Y, where I can have the wondrous
pleasure of walking around the gym for thirty minutes, around

and around and around in circles, until I'm so bored I'm
ready to scream.

So every year, I go through the same routine. In January, I'm full of vim and vigor as I head for the Y. By March,
I lose all my good intentions. The next thing I know it's Sep-
tember. By then, having forgotten why I quit exercising in
the spring, I just feel enormously guilty because I know how
important it is to get regular aerobic exercise. By December,
I'm once again determined to reform. I make my annual New
Year's resolution, believing for sure that this time I'll
keep it. And who knows? Maybe some year I will.

## 4   MORE ON DISCOVERY PROCEDURES

In Chapter 4, we considered the problems of finding a topic to write about
and deciding what to say about it. In that chapter, we discussed the use of *discovery
procedures*, ways of investigating a topic to discover something to say, and you were
introduced to one such discovery procedure—factor analysis. In this section, we
will examine some other discovery procedures.

Although you may not have been aware of it, in the last four chapters you've
learned how to use discovery procedures to explore topics in order to find main
ideas. In Chapter 3, you found that comparing and contrasting two similar things
could help you come up with a main idea. In Chapter 4, as you learned how to
defend a choice between two things, you were also learning to explore the process
of finding reasons you could use to justify your opinion on a topic. In Chapter 5,
as you read about how to write a classification composition, you were being
introduced to another way of investigating a topic—examining that topic to discover categories that you could discuss in a composition. In this chapter, you were
introduced to advantages and disadvantages as a way of exploring a topic.

To see how you can use these discovery procedures, let's assume you are
thinking about writing an essay on the general topic of bosses, but you aren't sure
what main idea you want to develop. You can use discovery procedures in order
to develop a number of possible main ideas. You can try choosing two bosses to
compare and contrast. Or you can consider writing an essay in which you defend
your opinion that one boss is better than another. You can also explore the possibility of explaining why you think one particular individual is a good boss or
another person a bad one. Or you can try to develop a classification of bosses into

three or more categories. Finally, you can choose one boss and examine that person's advantages (good qualities) and disadvantages (bad qualities). As you try those discovery procedures, the chances are good that you will find at least one main idea you can develop into an essay.

For another example, imagine that a professor asks you to write an essay on friendship, and you have no idea how to get started. Again, you can use the discovery procedures. You can try to compare and contrast two friendships in your life. You can explore the possibility of writing an essay to explain why you think one person is a better friend than another person, why one person is a wonderful friend, or why another is two-faced. For another example, you could try to develop a classification composition on kinds of friends. Finally, you could explore the advantages and disadvantages of a particular friendship. As you use those discovery procedures to investigate the topic, the chances are very good that you will find that indeed you can make some observations on that topic. When that happens, you will know the pleasure writers feel when they discover something they didn't know they knew.

## COMPOSITION ASSIGNMENT

Pick one of the ideas you developed in the journal assignment at the end of Section 2 and develop it into a composition in which you fully explore the good and bad characteristics of your topic. Use any or all of the discovery procedures you have learned about thus far to help you find ideas to include in your composition. Be sure to incorporate readers' signposts to help your reader follow your reasoning, and also be sure to proofread your composition carefully before turning it in.

## 5   SENTENCE COMBINING IN WRITTEN ENGLISH: CAUSE-AND-EFFECT SENTENCES

For this final look at sentence combining, we will examine the use of some sentence connectors that are useful in any context but that you may find especially handy in discussing the advantages and disadvantages of something. In advantage-and-disadvantage reasoning, you often have to think about the possible effect of some course of action: what good or bad outcome might that specific course of action cause? When you ask these questions, you are engaging in cause-and-effect thinking.

We engage in this kind of reasoning all the time. You can use a number of sentence connectors to combine sentences in order to show a cause-and-effect relationship. Suppose you wanted to combine these two sentences:

**Wages do not increase as fast as prices. Inflation is a terrible problem.**

The first sentence explains why inflation is such a terrible problem. It is the *cause*, and the second sentence is the *effect*. Given what you already know about spoken English, you would probably combine these sentences in one of the following three ways:

Inflation is a terrible problem *because* wages do not increase as fast as prices.

*Because* wages do not increase as fast as prices, inflation is a terrible problem.

Wages do not increase as fast as prices, *so* inflation is a terrible problem.

The connecting words *because* and *so* signal that these sentences show a cause-and-effect relationship. As you can tell from these examples, *because* is a two-place connector, and *so* is a comma connector.

These sentences can be combined in at least four ways to show cause and effect using semicolon connectors that are quite common in written English. Consider the following sentences:

Wages do not increase as fast as prices; *therefore*, inflation is a terrible problem.

Wages do not increase as fast as prices; *consequently*, inflation is a terrible problem.

Wages do not increase as fast as prices; *as a result*, inflation is a terrible problem.

Wages do not increase as fast as prices; *hence*, inflation is a terrible problem.

The words *therefore, consequently, as a result,* and *hence* are all used to mean *so* and to connect a cause with an effect. In addition, these words can be punctuated using a period, a capital letter, and a comma, as the following sentences illustrate:

Wages do not increase as fast as prices. *Therefore*, inflation is a terrible problem.

Wages do not increase as fast as prices. *As a result*, inflation is a terrible problem.

There is still another possible way of combining these sentences by using the comma connector *for*.

Inflation is a terrible problem, *for* wages do not increase as fast as prices.

This comma connector, which is almost never used in spoken English, can be used in written English when you want to discuss the effect first and then explain the cause.

## Sentence-Combining Practice

➤ Combine each pair of sentences in at least two ways. First, determine which sentence is the cause and which is the effect. Then use the patterns for cause-and-effect connecting words with correct punctuation. By the time you finish this exercise, you should have used all the connecting words that mean cause and effect.

1. I have too much homework. I can't go to the movie tonight.

   _____

   _____

2. My car is falling apart. I must buy a new one.

   _____

   _____

3. Madeline is always broke. She spends money foolishly.

   _____

   _____

4. Steve's wallet was stolen. He has no money.

   _____

   _____

5. Charles hates math. He failed the final exam in algebra.

   _____

   _____

6. Marvin's brother is seven feet tall. He is a fine basketball player.

_____

_____

7. James had studied for hours. The biology exam seemed easy.

_____

_____

8. Inez understands everything about history. The professor asked her to be a tutor.

_____

_____

9. Brenda goes to the library for two hours every day. She likes to study between classes.

_____

_____

10. Miguel is in excellent physical condition. He goes jogging five miles every day.

_____

_____

## Sentence-Creating Practice

➤ Write ten sentences of your own in which you use cause-and-effect sentence connectors. Try to use all the cause-and-effect connectors that you have been introduced to in this section.

1. _____

_____

2. _____

_____

3. _____

_____

4. _____

_____

5. _____

_____

6. _____

_____

7. _____

_____

8. _____

_____

9. _____

_____

10. _____

_____

## 6   SENTENCE COMBINING: PUTTING IT TOGETHER

➤ On your own paper, combine each group of sentences into one sentence. For some of the sentences, you will want to use cause-and-effect connectors. But not all of your sentences will make cause-and-effect points, so be prepared to use any of the sentence connectors you have already learned.

As you combine the sentences, group them into paragraphs and add readers' signposts as you would if you were writing this selection as a composition.

## A PERSON I HAVE TO TOLERATE

1. I wish I lived in an ideal world.
2. An ideal world is a perfect place.
3. The perfect place is filled with people.
4. The people are really nice.

5. I live in the real world.
6. The real world is an imperfect place.
7. That imperfect place has people.
8. The people are not very nice.

9. There's one person in particular.
10. She constantly gets on my nerves.

11. That person is Bertha.
12. She is my sister-in-law.

13. Bertha is one of those people.
14. They seem very nice at first.
15. We get to know them better.
16. We discover they are not what they seem.

17. Bertha looks like a cover girl on a magazine.
18. She is a gorgeous woman.
19. She has dark curly hair.
20. She has warm brown eyes.
21. She has an hourglass figure.

22. She looks so beautiful.
23. Everyone wants to meet her.

24. They meet her.
25. They love her.

26. She has a great sense of humor.
27. She knows a lot of jokes.
28. She's very witty.

29. People keep telling me.
30. I am so lucky.
31. Bertha is my sister-in-law.

32. I clench my teeth.
33. I try to smile.
34. I say nothing.

35. She is my favorite brother's wife.
36. I don't want to cause trouble in the family.
37. I don't say, "Looks can be deceiving."

38. Deep down inside I'm furious.
39. I really dislike Bertha.
40. I have two good reasons.

41. Bertha is extremely lazy.
42. She refuses to get a job.
43. She cannot find a job.
44. The job would let her sleep until noon every day.

45. She stays home most of the day.
46. The place always looks like a mess.

47. She hates to wash dishes.
48. Her sink is always full of dirty dishes.
49. Her sink is my brother's sink.

50. Her apartment is always dirty.
51. Her apartment is my brother's apartment.
52. She doesn't like to dust the furniture.
53. She doesn't like to vacuum the rug.
54. She doesn't like to mop the floor.

55. She says those jobs are boring.
56. I think she is just too lazy to do housework.

57. I dislike Bertha.
58. She cannot be trusted.

59. She smiles a lot to your face.
60. She talks about you behind your back.

61. Let me give you an example.
62. It will explain what she is really like.

63. I first met Bertha.
64. My friend Margie introduced us.

65. Bertha seemed very nice.
66. We became friends.
67. I introduced her to my brother.
68. They fell in love.
69. They got married.

70. A month later, Bertha and I were having lunch with two people.
71. They didn't know Margie very well.
72. One of them said that she had met Margie.

73. Bertha told her to be careful around Margie.
74. Margie used people.

75. I was amazed.
76. I thought Bertha liked Margie.

77. A few weeks later I saw Bertha.
78. She was talking to Margie.

79. Bertha was smiling.
80. She was laughing.
81. She was acting like a friend.

82. Then I understood Bertha is a two-faced person.
83. She cannot be trusted.

84. Bertha seems very nice.
85. You get to know her well.
86. You will discover her faults.

87. She is lazy.
88. She cannot be trusted.
89. You can understand why I don't like her.

90. Unfortunately, I have to tolerate her.
91. She is my favorite brother's wife.

# 7   USING WHAT YOU HAVE LEARNED IN OTHER WRITING ASSIGNMENTS

In this last section in Part I, we will discuss how to apply what you've learned about advantages and disadvantages to writing problems you encounter elsewhere. We will also discuss ways of using what you've learned about discovery procedures in assignments for academic courses.

First, let's consider ways to apply your knowledge of advantages and disadvantages to writing assignments you're given in other courses. The advantages and disadvantages format, which might also be called the "strengths and weaknesses" format, will be quite useful to you in many courses you take. For instance, suppose you're taking a course in political science, and the professor assigns a book review. You can discuss the good points of the book, its advantages or strengths, and then you can consider the bad points, its disadvantages or weaknesses. You can also use this format in essay examinations. If you're taking a course in recent U.S. history and you're asked to discuss Richard Nixon's presidency, you can discuss the positive accomplishments of his administration and then consider the negative aspects.

In addition, this format will be useful outside the academic world. If you have a job as an accountant, your boss might ask you to evaluate a new software package for computing federal income tax. You can discuss the advantages and disadvantages of the software. Or perhaps you work for a restaurant chain, and your supervisor asks you to evaluate a possible site for a new restaurant. You can present the strengths of the site and then its weaknesses.

Now we need to consider ways of applying what you've learned about discovery procedures to writing assignments in other courses. Imagine a professor asks you to write a research paper on some issue related to elderly people, and you have no idea how to choose an issue that you can easily develop into a paper. If you use the discovery procedures you have learned about in this book, you can explore the topic of the elderly in order to find such an issue.

For instance, you can consider writing a comparison and contrast paper in which you examine the way the elderly are treated in two different cultures. Or you might think about writing a classification paper in which you discuss different categories of elderly people in the United States. Finally, you could consider both the advantages and disadvantages of medical advances that have made it possible for more people to live to a ripe old age.

To consider another possible topic, suppose you want to write a paper on pollution, and your professor tells you that the topic is too big. How can you limit the topic to a more manageable size? You can use the discovery procedures to help you find a smaller topic related to pollution. You could compare and contrast the pollution problems in two cities or two countries. Through classification, you could discuss the kinds of pollution we need to worry about. Finally, you could consider both the advantages and disadvantages of policies that try to force factory owners to help clean up the environment.

In conclusion, the techniques you've acquired in this chapter will be valuable tools that you can use as you proceed through your course work. They will also be useful when you leave the university and enter the nonacademic world of work. As you make use of these techniques and others you've learned about in this book, you will come to know the pleasure of writing.

## Extra Writing Practice

➤ List a number of topics that have been discussed in some of the academic courses you've taken this term. First, develop main ideas for advantage and disadvantage essays on some of those topics. Then choose a few of those topics to see how you could apply the various discovery procedures in order to help you focus your thinking in order to plan and develop papers on those subjects.

# Part II

# AN INTRODUCTION TO THE GRAMMAR OF WRITTEN ENGLISH

## SEVEN

# GRAMMAR AS A GAME

### EXERCISE 1: THINKING ABOUT GRAMMAR

When you think of the word *grammar,* what images come into your mind? Do you think of hundreds of nouns, verbs, and adjectives marching across a page, putting you to sleep, or do you see a teacher frowning at you for not watching your grammar? Perhaps you imagine a big hole you fall into whenever you try to write. The one thing you probably don't think of is a game with rules that are easy to understand—like Monopoly or checkers or basketball or volleyball.

You may well be skeptical of any suggestion that grammar can be viewed as a game with rules that are easy to understand. If there is one thing you've discovered about grammar, it's that it is never easy. You may also doubt the wisdom of anyone who tells you that grammar is a game because games are supposed to be fun.

Given what your experience in school may have been, your doubts are reasonable—certainly, a lot of people share them. However, the study of grammar does not have to be difficult and unpleasant. It can be easy and enjoyable.

Let's begin by thinking about what grammar is. In the space below, write a definition for the word.

_____

_____

_____

If you are having difficulty defining it, it may not be your fault. Your teachers may never have told you what grammar is. In the simplest possible terms, grammar may be defined as a way of talking about language, a way of describing language. It is a tool that you and your teacher can use to talk about your problems and your strengths with written English. Talking about your problems is the first step toward solving them. The second step will come when you apply these concepts to your own writing as you proofread your compositions.

Now that you have some idea of what grammar is, let's return to the suggestion that it is a game with easily understood rules. To master this section of the book, you only have to be able to do one thing: you need to know how to play games with rules that must be followed. If you are good at grasping the concept of a rule in a game, then you will have no trouble learning the grammar in this book.

## EXERCISE 2: RECOGNIZING VERBS

Let's begin our study of how the game of grammar works by discussing a grammatical concept that you may be familiar with—verbs. Earlier in your schooling, you may have been taught the following definition: "Verbs express action or states of being." Because you know what verbs are, you should have no trouble identifying the verb in each of the following sentences. For these sentences, write the verb in the space at the right.

1. Steve played the piano.                        _____

2. Maria washed the dishes.                     _____

3. Helen took a walk.                               _____

In sentences 1 and 2, you probably didn't have any trouble deciding that *played* and *washed* are the verbs, but what is the verb in sentence 3? Is it *took* or *walk*? *Walk* certainly seems to express an action, but *took* can also do so (for example, *Helen took a sandwich*). So which one is the verb? As long as you try to use a definition for a verb that says a verb expresses an action, you will find sentences like sentence 3 difficult.

Let's see if we can come up with a better definition for verbs. Let's start with sentence 1, *Steve played the piano*. Suppose we change the time of the sentence to *right now*.

Steve *played* the piano.

becomes

Steve *is playing* the piano right now.

Now change the time to tomorrow.

Steve *will play* the piano tomorrow.

Notice that only one part of the sentence changes when the time changes. Now consider sentences 2 and 3:

**Maria washed the dishes.**
**Helen took a walk.**

Rewrite these sentences with the time changed to right now:

_____

_____

Now rewrite them with the time changed to tomorrow:

_____

_____

When the time of the sentence changes, one part of the sentence changes—the *verb*. So we now have a new definition for a verb. *A verb is the part of the sentence that changes form when the time of the sentence changes.* Using this definition, we can formulate a set of rules that you can use to find the verb in a sentence:

> *Rule 1:* Decide which of the following time expressions goes best with the sentence you are examining:
>
> yesterday     now     tomorrow
>
> *Rule 2:* Then change the time of the sentence by substituting a different time expression and making other necessary changes.
>
> *Rule 3:* The part of the sentence that changes is the verb.

To see how these rules work, consider the following examples:

**José needs a haircut.**
    Rule 1: José needs a haircut now.
    Rule 2: José needed a haircut yesterday.
    Rule 3: *Needs* is the verb.

**The old woman kicked the dog.**
    Rule 1: The old woman kicked the dog yesterday.

Rule 2: The old woman is kicking the dog now.
Rule 3: *Kicked* is the verb.

**My mother will bake a cherry pie.**
Rule 1: My mother will bake a cherry pie tomorrow.
Rule 2: My mother baked a cherry pie yesterday.
Rule 3: *Will bake* is the verb.

➤ Using the three rules for recognizing verbs, identify and underline the verb in each of the following sentences. The first sentence has been done for you.

1. The doctor <u>gave</u> Jeremy a shot.

2. The professor seems sleepy.

3. Mary Ann locked the car.

4. The detective drives a Honda.

5. Potato salad will taste delicious with the chicken sandwich.

6. Tony answered the question correctly.

7. Love makes life wonderful.

8. Mohammed forgot the coffee.

9. The University of Alabama has a great football team.

10. The reporters went for a long drive.

11. The glass broke into a thousand pieces.

12. Paul loves Vicky.

13. Sue's father broiled a sirloin steak.

14. The secretaries are angry.

15. My brother needs a good kick in the seat of the pants.

16. That coat looks very expensive.

17. Jerry shaved off his beard.

18. Dorothy's boyfriend wanted an ice-cream cone.

19. My sister-in-law will sing at Ingrid's wedding.

20. This exercise is easy.

## EXERCISE 3: MORE ON VERBS: AUXILIARY VERBS

The three rules for verb recognition that we discussed in Exercise 2 will help you to identify the verb in most of the sentences that you are going to be dealing with. However, you would have some difficulty using our three-step rule with a few verb constructions. For example, look at the following sentences:

Sandra has gone to Pittsburgh.
Henry James has been sick.
Samson has shaved his beard.

With sentences like these, it is very difficult to apply Rule 1 and decide which time expression fits. In order to make our rules for verb recognition work with such sentences, we're going to have to revise our rule for verb recognition. We can do this very simply by adding a second part to Rule 1:

> *Rule 1a:* If you have difficulty deciding which time expression goes best with the sentence, look for any auxiliary verb construction in the sentence. That auxiliary verb construction will be the verb.

Before we can use Rule 1a, we must define *auxiliary verb construction.* To do so, let's go back to Exercise 2. In many of the examples we worked with in that exercise, when you applied Rule 2 and added the expression *right now,* you changed the verb form by breaking it into two words:

*played* became *is playing*
*washed* became *is washing*
*took* became *is taking*

Similarly, when you applied Rule 2 and added the expression *tomorrow,* two words resulted:

*played* became *will play*
*washed* became *will wash*
*took* became *will take*

As you may have already been taught, words like *is* and *will* are called *auxiliary verbs* (also sometimes called "helping verbs"). Auxiliary verbs can combine with *main verbs* (like *playing, washing, taking, play, wash,* and *take*) to form what we will call auxiliary verb constructions. *An auxiliary verb construction begins with a helping verb and ends with a main verb, and there may be one or two other helping verbs in the middle.*

If we look again at the sentences at the beginning of this exercise, we will discover the following auxiliary verb constructions:

Sandra *has gone* to Pittsburgh.
Henry James *has been* sick.
Samson *has shaved* his beard.

Here are some other examples of auxiliary verb constructions:

Jason *is drying* the dishes.
Anne *has moved* to Atlanta.
Regina *may drop* the class.
My sister *may add* that class.
Harry *should have left* the car keys.
Melissa *may have been waiting* for three hours.

In case you have trouble recognizing auxiliary verbs, here is a complete list of the auxiliary verbs in English:

| Forms of *be* | | Forms of *have* | Forms of *do* | Modal Auxiliaries | |
|---|---|---|---|---|---|
| am | was | has | do | can | could |
| are | were | have | does | may | might |
| is | being | had | did | shall | should |
| be | been | | | will | would |
| | | | | must | |

You may find two kinds of sentences rather tricky when you are searching for auxiliary verb constructions. One is a sentence that asks a question. Questions are deceptive in English because the auxiliary verb construction is divided into two parts:

*Will* Heather *find* true love?
*Has* Frank *discovered* the truth?

*Did* the students *enjoy* the biology class?
Where *will* you *leave* the car?

In the other kind of problem sentence, certain words break the auxiliary verb construction into two parts:

I *have* never *eaten* sushi.
Jeremy *does* not *enjoy* ice hockey.
Susan *will* always *be searching* for an honest man.

Words like *never, not,* and *always,* which interrupt the auxiliary verb constructions, are not part of the verb because their form never changes regardless of the time of the sentence.

➤ Using Rules 1, 1a, 2, and 3, identify and underline the verb in each of the following sentences. The first sentence has been done for you.

1. My cats <u>are</u> <u>scratching</u> the sofa.

2. Her little brother grew six inches last summer.

3. Ronnie has been sick for a week.

4. Did you study for the test?

5. His red Porsche has disappeared.

6. Juan must speak English.

7. This piano sounds terrible.

8. Jennifer is beautiful.

9. Maureen talks too much.

10. Will the Democrats win the next presidential election?

11. Kevin knows everything about cars.

12. Adam was late.

13. My sister and her fiancé were invited to that party.

14. The suspect was captured at the corner of Hollywood and Vine.

15. Maria had never seen snow before.

16. Abby has never been on time.

17. The garlic chicken tastes delicious.

18. Michael has been reading that book for a month.

19. Are Aunt Martha and Uncle Toby coming to dinner?

20. Where did all the food go?

## EXERCISE 4: RECOGNIZING SUBJECTS

Now that you have learned how to recognize verbs in sentences, you are ready to learn how to recognize *subjects*. In the past, you may have been told that the subject is "what the sentence is about." Consider the following sentence:

**The old woman fixed the flat tire.**

What is this sentence about? Is it about the old woman, is it about the tire, or is it about the old woman fixing the tire?

Obviously, we need to find a better way of determining which part of the sentence is the subject. As you might expect, given what you learned in Exercises 2 and 3, we are going to identify the subject of a sentence by using rules. We will use the following rules:

> *Rule 4:* Find the verb.
>
> *Rule 5a:* If the sentence is a question, the subject will be between the two parts of the verb.
>
> *Rule 5b:* If the sentence is not a question, ask *who* or *what* "does" the verb.
>
> *Rule 5c:* The answer to the question in Rule 5b will be the subject for sentences that are not questions.

To see how the rules work, let's consider the following examples:

**The old woman fixed the flat tire.**
> Rule 4: *Fixed* is the verb.
> Rule 5b: Who fixed it? The old woman.
> Rule 5c: *The old woman* is the subject.

**The basketball was thrown across the gym.**
> Rule 4: *Was thrown* is the verb.
> Rule 5b: What was thrown? The basketball.
> Rule 5c: *The basketball* is the subject.

**Will the movie end at 3:00 P.M.?**
> Rule 4: *Will end* is the verb.
> Rule 5a: *The movie* is the subject.

**The prince was tricked by the wicked witch.**
> Rule 4: *Was tricked* is the verb.
> Rule 5b: Who was tricked? The prince.
> Rule 5c: *The prince* is the subject.

➤ Using the rules for recognizing subjects, go back to the sentences in Exercise 2 (page 130) and Exercise 3 (page 133), and identify the subjects by circling them.

Now identify the subject and the verb in each of the following sentences. Circle the subject, and underline the verb. The first sentence has been done for you.

1. Michael Jordan is my idol.

2. My radio and my stereo were stolen.

3. The president should lead us.

4. When did you come to this country?

5. Santa Claus gave Dr. Joyce Brothers a kiss.

6. The children are playing in the street.

7. Seth has always wanted a dog.

8. The roses need some water.

9. My car uses too much oil.

10. The pink panther chased a yellow elephant.

11. Elvis kissed Priscilla on the cheek.

12. Do you like this record?

13. My aunt tells us about all her ailments.

14. Harvey joined the Marines yesterday.

15. Mr. Higgins is losing his mind.

16. Has Virginia been visiting her mother at the nursing home?

17. Maurice may write his composition tonight.

18. This building should get a new roof.

19. The mayor and the governor had a disagreement.

20. Can anyone help us?

# EIGHT

# Defining the Sentence: Recognizing and Correcting Fragments

**N**ow that you are familiar with the idea of following rules in order to identify subjects and verbs, you are ready to use this approach to learn how to recognize *good sentences* in written English. When you talk, you don't have to worry about whether you have produced a good sentence as opposed to a *fragment* or a *run-on sentence*. But when you write, you do have to worry because fragments and run-ons are not good sentences in written English.

Let's begin our discussion with what you already know about sentences. Years ago you learned that a good sentence is "a group of words that express a complete thought." If this rule is to be useful in recognizing fragments and run-ons, we will have to figure out what a "complete thought" is. In the space below, explain what you think a complete thought is.

_____

_____

_____

Chances are that you are finding it very difficult to explain what the phrase means, and that difficulty is understandable. Even if you were a professor of English, you would have a hard time explaining the phrase. It is extremely difficult, if not impossible, to define. We will have to find a better rule for recognizing good sentences.

Unfortunately, however, it is very difficult to develop a simple rule to define a good sentence in written English, so you will have to be patient as we develop a series of rules, in this chapter and the next, that will help you to recognize the differences between good and bad sentences.

## EXERCISE 1: GOOD SENTENCES VERSUS FRAGMENTS

When you are writing compositions, you have to make decisions about when to end a sentence by using a period. If you are not sure about the rules for good sentences in written English, you may end up writing *fragments*—pieces of sentences that are mistakenly punctuated as if they were good sentences.

To help you learn to recognize the difference between fragments and good sentences, let's begin by considering the following examples:

Went to the store.
Maria is walking the dog.
The boy on the corner.
The professor is in her office.

Which ones are good sentences? Which ones are fragments, pieces of sentences? How would you turn the fragments into good sentences?

_____

_____

Examples like these help us to define our first rule about how good sentences differ from fragments.

> *Rule 6:* A good sentence must have a subject and a verb; therefore, a group of words with no subject or no verb will be a fragment.

➤ Using Rule 6, proofread the following examples. Which are good sentences, and which are fragments? Correct the fragments by adding either a subject or a verb, or, if necessary, both a subject and a verb. Write "C" (for "correct") after any good sentences you find. The first fragment has been corrected for you.

1. *I*
   ⌃Am taking Chemistry 101.

2. John swept the floor.

3. The girl in the brown sweater.

4. She sneezed.

5. Over the river and through the woods.

6. The man with the cocker spaniel.

7. Was pushing my car on Halsted.

8. Biology is very interesting.

9. The buses are running late today.

10. Slipped on the ice and broke her leg.

11. Last night at Wrigley Field.

12. The girl in the alley has a new ball.

13. Is not true.

14. A group of words with no subject.

15. I will not study tonight.

In this exercise, you have practiced correcting a fragment by adding a subject or a verb (and sometimes by adding both a subject and a verb). Now you need to learn how to use what you've learned when you are proofreading your compositions for fragments.

Let's begin by considering the following examples:

**We drove the car. To a park beside the river.**
**Bill found the book. On a table in the cafeteria.**

In each of these examples, the first group of words is a good sentence, but the second group is a fragment that needs both a subject and a verb. If you examine the examples carefully, you will guess that the best way to add a subject and a verb to these fragments is to add the fragments to the good sentences, as in the following examples:

**We drove the car to a park beside the river.**
**Bill found the book on a table in the cafeteria.**

These examples show that one way of correcting a fragment is to add it to a good sentence.

Now let's consider another fragment problem that you may need to correct when you're proofreading. Consider the following examples:

**The man in the blue shirt. Wants a ride to work.**
**The woman with the German shepherd. Was my biology teacher**
    **last year.**

Each of these examples contains two fragments. The first group of words needs a verb, and the second needs a subject. How can you correct them? As you might have guessed, the best solution is to put the two fragments together to make a good sentence. For example:

**The man in the blue shirt wants a ride to work.**
**The woman with the German shepherd was my biology teacher**
    **last year.**

So, when you're correcting a fragment in your composition, you should check to see if it is possible to attach the fragment either to a good sentence or to another fragment in order to create one long good sentence. If you can correct the fragment in that way, then you have found the best solution. If you cannot use this method, then you will have to add whatever is necessary to turn the fragment into a good sentence.

➤ Proofread the following examples, correcting the fragments by using what you have learned in this exercise. Write "C" (for "correct") after any pairs of good sentences. The first sentence has been done for you.

16. The plane from Poland will ~~land. In~~ *land in* an hour or two.

17. The students enjoyed the class. They didn't hear the bell.

18. A black cat with white tips on its ears. Climbed up on the fence.

19. You can have the book. From now until the end of the term.

20. A beautiful woman with curly black hair. Asked Herman for a date.

21. My baby cried all night long. Am very tired this morning.

22. Francesca made a German chocolate cake. Oscar ate half of it.

23. You can see my grandmother in the picture. With her children around her.

24. The dog was covered with flour. From his nose to his tail.

25. A tall blond man ran up the escalator. He was wearing one brown shoe.

26. Is raining today. We won't be able to have the picnic.

27. The brick mansion in the middle of the block. Belongs to the governor.

## EXERCISE 2: FRAGMENT PROBLEMS WITH SENTENCE CONNECTORS

In your work with sentence connectors in the first part of this book, you will learn that many words can be used to connect sentences. You need to be aware that it's possible to misuse some of those connecting words in a way that will produce sentence fragments.

Consider the following examples:

Robert doesn't enjoy playing basketball. *Because he hates to run.*
*If you proofread your compositions carefully.* You won't make so many mistakes.
*When the teacher walked into the room.* The students quit talking.

The italicized groups of words in these sentences do have a subject and a verb, but they are not good sentences in written English. To understand why, you need to become familiar with the difference between *independent clauses* and *dependent clauses*.

First, we need to define the term *clause*: *A clause is a group of words that has a subject and a verb.* Here are some examples of clauses:

The infant was crying loudly.
Because my brother is lazy.
This book is easy to read.
When I leave the room.

Some clauses are *independent clauses* and can be punctuated as sentences in written English, but other clauses are *dependent clauses* and cannot be punctuated as sentences. The easiest way for you to tell the difference between them is to learn to recognize dependent clauses. Then you will be able to recognize independent clauses because all other clauses are independent.

Certain connecting words always come at the beginning of a dependent clause. One kind of connecting word that begins a dependent clause is the *two-place connector*. (In some textbooks, two-place connectors are called *subordinating conjunctions*.) Two-place connectors can appear at the beginning of either the first clause or the second clause, as in the following sentences:

*Because* Robert hates to run, he doesn't enjoy playing basketball.
Robert doesn't enjoy playing basketball *because* he hates to run.

*If* you proofread your compositions carefully, you won't make so many mistakes.
You won't make so many mistakes *if* you proofread your compositions carefully.

*When* the teacher walked into the room, the students quit talking.
The students quit talking *when* the teacher walked into the room.

Because two-place connectors form dependent clauses, you cannot place a period between the two clauses. If you do, you will produce a fragment. Consider the following examples:

*Because* Robert hates to run. He doesn't enjoy playing basketball.
You won't make so many mistakes. *If* you proofread your compositions carefully.
The students quit talking. *When* the teacher walked into the room.

The italicized words are two-place connectors, and they mark the clauses that follow them as dependent clauses which cannot be punctuated as good sentences in written English.

To avoid producing this kind of sentence, we need the following rule:

> *Rule 7:* A clause that begins with a two-place connector is a dependent clause. So when you are using two-place connectors to combine sentences, you should never use a period between the two clauses. If the two-place connector comes at the beginning of the two clauses, put a comma before the second clause. If the two-place connector comes between the two clauses, use no punctuation mark at all.

To help you use this rule, here is a list of the most common two-place connectors in English.

| | | | |
|---|---|---|---|
| after | because | since | when |
| although | before | unless | while |
| as | if | until | |

➤ Using Rules 6 and 7, proofread the following examples, correcting the fragments. Write "C" (for "correct") after any examples that contain no fragments. The first one has been done for you.

1. The ice has melted. We can go fishing in the lake now.   *C*

2. Because the smoke burned the firemen's eyes. They had to leave the building.

3. It started a long time ago when I was very young.

4. Irma is a nice person. She helps me with my homework.

5. Although Bill hates biology. He intends to get an A in it.

6. While Jim was studying, his brother was taking a nap.

7. Gloria screamed. When she saw a snake.

8. Sonia spoke only Spanish until she started school.

9. When the baseball players went on strike. Dave became interested in soccer.

10. I always write fragments. I never write run-ons.

11. If you know the list of two-place connectors. You will find this exercise easy.

12. When you finish this exercise, you can have a break.

13. Before I came to college. I didn't know the difference between a fragment and a run-on.

14. Dorothy always writes run-on sentences. She never writes fragments.

15. My cat Tuptim took a nap after she ate her breakfast.

16. I'm too scared to jump out of the plane. Because my parachute may not open.

17. Since Cosmo hasn't slept for three days, he probably won't make it to the party tonight.

18. Sheena thinks that a tattoo is a smart investment. It lasts a lifetime.

19. If you agree to make me your vice-president. I will vote for you.

20. I won't vote for you unless you agree.

## EXERCISE 3: FRAGMENT PROBLEMS WITH RELATIVE PRONOUNS

In this exercise, we are going to consider another kind of connector that can begin a dependent clause—the *relative pronoun*. In English the words *who, which,* and *that* are relative pronouns and can be used to combine sentences.

The following examples are good sentences in written English:

Bill wants to marry a woman who has lots of money.
We found an Italian restaurant which serves fantastic ravioli.
Sue is reading a book that Ralph Ellison wrote.

However, if you punctuate these sentences in the following way, you will produce sentence fragments because you have punctuated dependent clauses as if they were sentences:

Bill wants to marry a woman. Who has lots of money.
We found an Italian restaurant. Which serves fantastic ravioli.
Sue is reading a book. That Ralph Ellison wrote.

To avoid producing fragments like these, we need the following rule:

> *Rule 8*: Clauses that begin with *relative pronouns* are dependent clauses, so they should not be punctuated as sentences. Instead, they should be attached to the independent clauses that come before them.

The rules that tell you when to use commas before relative pronouns and when not to are complex; however, in this exercise, we're going to use a simple rule. If the relative pronoun comes after the name of a person or a place, use a comma before the relative pronoun. If the relative pronoun does not come after the name of a person or place, do *not* use a comma before the relative pronoun.

➤ **Proofread the following examples using Rule 8, correcting any fragments you find. Write "C" (for "correct") after any example that contains no mistakes. The first sentence has been done for you.**

1.  Bill wants to marry Helen ~~Rogers. Who~~ <u>Rogers, who</u> has a very rich father.

2.  He bought the desk that had belonged to her grandfather.

3.  Tom enjoyed his visit to Albany, which is the capital of New York.

4.  Sue grew up in Cape Girardeau. Which is a small town in Missouri.

5.  You should never swim in a lake. Which is polluted.

6.  Martha is looking for a doctor who is inexpensive.

7.  Sarah lives next door to Jane Byrne who was the mayor of Chicago.

8.  Michael hated the sweater. That Marjorie gave him for Christmas.

9.  The Hills are looking for a house which has a fireplace.

10. Cynthia doesn't believe the story. That he told.

## EXERCISE 4: REAL VERBS VERSUS FALSE VERBS

Some groups of words appear to be good sentences because they contain subjects and words that seem to be verbs. Consider the following examples:

**The boy walking down the street.** (*walking* seems to be a verb)
**The ball thrown through the window.** (*thrown* seems to be a verb)
**The girl to leave the room.** (*to leave* seems to be a verb)

But these words are not *real verbs*. They are *false verbs*.

Although there are several kinds of *false verbs,* in this exercise we're going to concentrate on three kinds:

1. An *-ing* form of a verb, like *walking* or *singing,* which does *not* have a form of *be* in front of it.
2. An *-n* or *-en* form of a verb, like *thrown* or *given,* which does *not* have a form of *be* in front of it.
3. An infinitive: the *to*-form of a verb; for example, *to run, to laugh, to play, to dance, to sing.*

Any time you see an infinitive, you know that you have a false verb. However, you have to be more careful about the other two kinds of false verbs because they are sometimes parts of real verbs. For example, an *-ing* word that does have a form of *be* in front of it is a real verb (*was walking, were leaving, are running, is going, am singing*). Similarly, an *-n* or *-en* form that does have a form of *be* in front of it is a real verb (*was thrown, were taken, is written*). (In addition, an *-en* form with a form of *have* in front of it is a real verb, as in *has driven, have written, had known.* However, because these *-en* forms are not usually a problem for recognizing fragments, we are going to ignore them.)

We are now ready for another rule that will help in distinguishing good sentences from fragments.

> *Rule 9:* A good sentence must have a subject and a real verb; any group of words that only has a false verb will be a fragment.

➤ Using Rule 9, proofread the following examples. Write "C" (for "correct") after the good sentences and "F" (for "fragment") after the fragments. The first sentence has been done for you.

1. The infant was crying loudly.  *C*

2. The potatoes eaten by the students.

3. The child playing in the yard.

4. The ball was thrown by the pitcher.

5. Maureen to sing at the wedding.

6. A car driven at a high rate of speed.

7. The lake frozen by zero degree weather.

8. The letter was written yesterday.

9. The student given a chance to learn.

10. Jim working on the car.

11. Mike is studying French.

12. Don to learn Italian in Rome.

13. The students were given a chance to learn.

14. Jill wants to study Spanish.

15. The story written by my brother.

16. The airplane circling the airport with one wing on fire.

Fragments like those you have just identified may be corrected in several ways. Some of the most common ways are shown below:

1. For *-ing* and *-en* fragments, you can add an appropriate form of *be* in front of the false verb in order to turn it into a real verb. For example:
   *The boy walking down the street*
   could be changed to
   *The boy is walking down the street.*
   *The ball thrown through the window*
   could be changed to
   *The ball was thrown through the window.*

2. For *-ing* and *-en* fragments, you can add a real verb along with any other words you might need at the end of the sentence. For instance:
   *The boy walking down the street*
   could be changed to
   *The boy walking down the street needs a haircut.*
   *The ball thrown through the window*
   could be changed to
   *The ball thrown through the window belongs to my brother.*

3. For *to-form* fragments, you can add a real verb between the subject and the infinitive form. For example:

   *The girl to leave the room*

   could be changed to

   *The girl wants to leave the room.*

4. For all three kinds of fragments, you can add a completely new verb and new subject at the beginning of the sentence.

   *The boy walking down the street*

   could be changed to

   *I watched the boy walking down the street.*

   *The ball thrown through the window*

   could be changed to

   *Steve saw the ball thrown through the window.*

   *The girl to leave the room*

   could be changed to

   *The teacher permitted the girl to leave the room.*

➤ Now, go back to the list of sentences and fragments you've just proofread, and correct each of the fragments which you identified.

## EXERCISE 5: COMMANDS VERSUS FRAGMENTS

As a general rule, most sentences in written English must have a subject and a real verb, but one kind of sentence appears to be an exception to this rule. Sentences that command the reader to do something usually do not have visible subjects. Look at the following sentences:

Look at the drawing on page 100.
Learn how to recognize false verbs.
Memorize the list of two-place connectors.
Read the essay on the next page.

With sentences like these, it seems to be difficult to apply our rules for recognizing subjects. But if you think about it, it is easy to figure out *who* is supposed to do the action of the verb—the person who is reading the sentence. Sentences like these that command the reader—*you*—to do something have an "understood" subject.

To distinguish commands like these from fragments, we need the following rule:

> *Rule 10:* For commands, the subject does not have to be named in the sentence. But for all other good sentences in written English, the subject must be named.

➤ Using Rule 10, proofread the following examples. Add words to turn all fragments into good sentences, and write "C" (for "correct") after all good sentences. The first sentence has been done for you.

1. <sub>she</sub> Was correcting the fragments.

2. Don't do this exercise carelessly.

3. Wants to drop the course.

4. Is angry.

5. Discover the answer by yourself.

6. Has found the answer.

7. Memorize the rules for good sentences.

8. Are getting excited about our trip.

9. Proofread every assignment carefully.

10. Doesn't care for classical music.

## EXERCISE 6: REVIEWING GOOD SENTENCES VERSUS FRAGMENTS

Review the five rules (Rules 6–10) for recognizing fragments before you do this exercise.

➤ Proofread the following examples, correcting any fragments you find. Write "C" (for "correct") after any examples that contain no fragments. The first sentence has been done for you.

1. The student carried the load of ~~books. From~~ *books from* Foster to Bryn Mawr.

2. Jane will go to New York with us if her husband lets her.

3. The student trying to find the cafeteria. Is hungry enough to eat stale potato chips.

4. Maria was born in Cuba. She now lives in Minneapolis.

5. Mrs. Davis is on vacation. And won't be back for two weeks.

6. Whenever Bill has a date with Eleanor, he is always an hour late.

7. The professor looking for a piece of chalk.

8. If money can't buy happiness. Why do so many people want money?

9. The woman with a purple coat and a brown plaid scarf. Is Bob's wife.

10. The man failed his driver's test. And is afraid to try again.

11. Since you learned to speak English, you have forgotten how to speak Chinese.

12. Don't count your chickens. Until they're hatched.

13. Louisa is looking for a turquoise dress. Which has a long skirt.

14. No one ever listens to him. Because his stories are very boring.

15. The guy driving the red Cadillac.

16. Susan bought a sweater. That her husband hates.

17. The boys are playing basketball in the park.

18. If you live in a glass house, you should not throw stones.

19. Don't ever underestimate the power of a woman.

20. The truck driven down the highway at a high rate of speed.

21. Mr. Evans the man to see.

22. Is true that students have a lot of work to do.

23. They yawned.

24. My cousin the biggest liar in the city of Cincinnati.

25. You should never drive a car that has bad brakes.

26. Is snowing on the south side of Chicago.

27. Karen is never on time.

28. Chen will never be a good tennis player because he never practices.

29. It is raining.

30. Because I know how to recognize fragments. This exercise was easy.

## EXERCISE 7: PROOFREADING FOR FRAGMENTS

➤ Proofread the following composition to correct sentence fragment errors. The first correction has been made for you.

WINTER IN MINNEAPOLIS

If you can survive a Minneapolis ~~winter. You~~ winter, you can survive almost anything. When the wind-chill is twenty degrees below zero. You know that you are in for trouble unless you learn how to battle the cold. What can you do to beat the wintry chill? Here are some tips.

First, you must learn how to dress warmly. To do this, you must forget about how you look. And think only about staying warm. One way to stay warm is to wear your clothes in layers. With a shirt and one or two sweaters under your coat. If you can afford to buy long underwear for your legs. You should do that too. When you go out, you may look like a fat polar bear, but don't worry about how you look.

Another important tip. In Minneapolis, you have to worry about frostbite. There are three areas on your body. Which frostbite can hit—your ears, hands, and feet. How to avoid frostbite? You should never go outside when it is below zero. Without a hat or scarf covering your ears. And warm gloves or mittens covering your hands. For your feet, you need some very warm socks and a pair of heavy insulated boots. When you are warmly dressed, you can go outside. Even if the wind-chill is twenty below.

If you want to stay as warm as possible. You need to learn a few more tricks. You must learn to avoid standing on the corner. Waiting for the bus. How can you do this? It helps if you live close to a bus stop. Because you can wait until you see the bus coming. Then you can leave the house. And hurry to the bus stop. If you don't live close to a bus stop. You must find a doorway. Which can protect you from the wind. If you can't find a doorway, you must keep moving. You should walk back and forth. Stamping your feet. Is true that some people may think you're crazy. But you won't care because you will be warm.

If you follow my advice. You are sure to survive a winter in Minneapolis. You only have one other choice. You can move to a place like Florida. Which is always warm.

## EXERCISE 8: PROOFREADING TIP ON USING COMMAS WITH INTRODUCTORY PHRASES

In spoken English, you never have to worry about when to use commas, but in written work commas do present a problem. There are specific rules that tell you where you are supposed to use commas and where you are not; however, the rules for comma usage are very complex.

You can master these rules by concentrating on learning them one at a time. As you work through the exercises in Parts I and II of this book, you will be introduced to many comma rules. If you learn each rule as it is introduced, by the time you finish this book you will be well on your way to becoming an expert in comma usage.

In Exercise 2 in this chapter, you learned that with two-place connectors, whenever a dependent clause comes *before* an independent clause, you should use a comma to separate the two clauses. The following examples show this usage:

**Before the movie ended, Maritza fell asleep.**
**Although Greg didn't study, he made an A on the test.**

In this exercise, we will consider a similar comma rule for *phrases* that come *before* independent clauses—for phrases that *introduce* independent clauses.

Consider the following sentences:

**In the middle of the park, an elderly man was flying a kite.**
**To recognize fragments, you must be able to recognize a subject**
      **and a verb.**
**A few feet away from the tent, Kathy saw a raccoon.**

These sentences begin with *phrases,* groups of words with no subjects and no real verbs. These phrases come before the independent clauses. Notice that a comma is used to separate the phrase from an independent clause. Here are some more examples:

**In Mary's opinion, Professor Bofman should be given a big raise.**
**In linguistics, we study the structure and history of languages.**
**Before the end of class, the instructor returned our tests.**

To summarize what you've learned in this exercise, we can use the following rule:

> *Rule 11:* Whenever a phrase comes *before* an independent clause, use a comma to separate the phrase and the clause.

➤ Use what you have learned in this exercise to proofread the following sentences, adding commas where necessary. Write "C" after any sentences that are correct. The first sentence has been done for you.

1. In my opinion, Kuwait was not worth a war.   *C*

2. Near the lakeshore a young man was standing.

3. We will go to a movie after the final exam.

4. During the meeting the committee will consider your proposal.

5. To understand Martha, you must get to know her mother.

6. After swimming across the lake we went for a walk along the shore.

7. My car had a flat tire two blocks from the house.

8. From now until June we will be planning the wedding.

9. To avoid colds you should take lots of Vitamin C.

10. In biology we study the various forms of plant and animal life.

11. Before the test, Barbara will lend you her notes.

12. After an introductory phrase you should always use a comma.

# NINE

# Defining the Sentence: Recognizing and Correcting Run-ons

In the previous chapter we looked at the sentence fragment, a type of error that results when a subject or a verb is missing from a sentence. In this chapter we will consider the other most common kind of sentence error, the run-on. A run-on is not missing a subject or a verb; instead, it is an error that results when two or more clauses are combined in a sentence without the necessary connector or punctuation marks.

## EXERCISE 1: GOOD SENTENCES VERSUS RUN-ONS: USING COMMA CONNECTORS

When you are combining two or more sentences into one sentence, you will usually find that there are several possible ways you can do it. However, you should be aware that you *cannot* do either of two things when you are combining sentences: (1) You cannot string them together with a comma between them. (2) You cannot string them together with nothing between them.

For example, consider the following sentences:

My car wouldn't start. I took the bus to school.
Sue finds Jim boring. She goes out with him anyway.
John will bring soda. Mary will bring chips.

These sentences can be combined in a number of ways:

My car wouldn't start, so I took the bus to school.
Because my car wouldn't start, I took the bus to school.
My car wouldn't start; therefore, I took the bus to school.

Sue finds Jim boring, but she goes out with him anyway.
Although Sue finds Jim boring, she goes out with him anyway.
Sue finds Jim boring; however, she goes out with him anyway.

John will bring soda, and Mary will bring chips.
John will bring soda; in addition, Mary will bring chips.

These sentences *cannot* be combined in the following ways:

My car wouldn't start, I took the bus to school.
My car wouldn't start I took the bus to school.

Sue finds Jim boring, she goes out with him anyway.
Sue finds Jim boring she goes out with him anyway.

John will bring soda, Mary will bring chips.
John will bring soda Mary will bring chips.

If you produce sentences like these last six, you will have produced *run-on sentences.*

What is a run-on sentence? How does it differ from a good sentence in written English? To answer these questions, we need to examine the sentences above very carefully. What makes the first group of sentences different from the second group? As you can probably guess, the words *so, because, therefore, but, although, however, and,* and *in addition* make the first group different from the second one. All these words are sentence connectors, as you will learn as you work with the chapters in Part I of this book.

Now we can use what we've learned to develop a rule that will help distinguish between good sentences and run-ons.

> *Rule 12:* You can combine two sentences into one sentence by using *sentence connectors.* If you string two sentences together without using a sentence connector, you will produce a run-on.

If you are going to use this rule, you will need to have some rules that define sentence connectors. Let's begin with a rule defining one kind of sentence connector you are already familiar with:

## EXERCISE 2: GOOD SENTENCES VERSUS RUN-ONS: USING TWO-PLACE CONNECTORS

In this exercise, we're going to consider the use of *two-place connectors*—a group of sentence connectors that were discussed in Chapter 8, Exercise 2. Consider the following sentences:

Although Sue finds Jim boring, she goes out with him.
Sue goes out with Jim although she finds him boring.

Because my car wouldn't start, I took the bus to school.
I took the bus to school because my car wouldn't start.

If Steve goes to the party, Mary will go.
Mary will go to the party if Steve goes.

As you can see, the words *if, although,* and *because* can be placed in the middle of the two sentences that are being combined, or they can be placed at the very beginning of the two sentences.

At this point we're ready to add a third rule you can use when you are trying to tell the difference between good sentences and run-ons:

> *Rule 14: Two-place connectors* are a second kind of sentence connector. When a two-place connector comes at the very beginning of the two sentences you are combining, put a comma before the second sentence. When a two-place connector comes in the middle of the two sentences that are being combined, don't use any punctuation at all. (In some books, *two-place connectors* are called *subordinating conjunctions.*)

To make it easier for you to use Rule 14, here is a list of some common two-place connectors in English:

| | | | |
|---|---|---|---|
| after | because | since | when |
| although | before | unless | while |
| as | if | until | |

➤ Using Rules 12 and 14, proofread the following examples. Correct the run-ons by adding two-place connectors. Write "C" after any sentence that is correct. The first sentence has been done for you.

1. Because it hasn't rained in two months, the crops are dying. *C*

2. I need to buy a new coat, mine is falling apart.

3. My friend Bill came along in his car while we were waiting for a bus.

4. Walter cooked dinner, his wife read the newspaper.

5. If you dust the furniture, I'll vacuum the rug.

6. We burned the leaves after we raked them.

7. Before we went to bed, we watched the eclipse of the moon.

8. I didn't study for the test, I made an A.

9. My father wants to move to Arizona because he hates ice and snow.

10. Barry got up at 5:30, he took a shower.

11. Although Margie writes beautiful poetry, she is failing Writing 101.

12. Gretchen was washing the dishes, the phone rang.

13. Sarita lived in Puerto Rico until she was eleven years old.

14. Sue's boyfriend is very handsome, he's very stupid.

15. As Jane was walking down the street, she slipped on a banana peel.

## EXERCISE 3: GOOD SENTENCES WITH SEMICOLON CONNECTORS

In this exercise, we're going to consider a group of sentence connectors that are not often used in the spoken English most of us use. They are very common in written English, so you should become familiar with them.

Let's begin by considering the following sentences that use comma connectors:

My coat is falling apart, so I need to buy a new one.
Some people like baseball, but other people prefer football.
My brother is very handsome, and he is very intelligent.

Now consider the following sentences:

> My coat is falling apart; therefore, I need to buy a new one.
> Some people like baseball; however, other people prefer football.
> My brother is very handsome; moreover, he is very intelligent.

The second group of sentences contains what we are going to call *semicolon connectors* (words like *therefore, however,* and *moreover*), which can be used to join two sentences if a semicolon is put in front of the connector and a comma is added after the connector.

Even if you are not familiar with the words *therefore, however,* and *moreover,* you can probably guess from the examples above that *therefore* means the same thing as *so, however* means the same as *but,* and *moreover* means the same thing as *and.*

Now you are ready for the fourth rule to be used in distinguishing between run-ons and good sentences.

---

*Rule 15: Semicolon connectors* are a third kind of sentence connector. When you use them to combine two sentences, always put a semicolon before the connector and a comma after the connector. If you don't use a semicolon before the connector, you will produce a run-on sentence. (In some books, *semicolon connectors* are called *adverbial conjunctions.*)

---

➤ Using Rules 12 and 15, proofread the following sentences, correcting the run-ons by adding semicolon connectors. Write "C" after any sentences that are correct. The first sentence has been done for you.

1. I did the exercise ~~carelessly,~~ *carelessly; therefore,* I made some foolish mistakes.

2. Sue didn't study for the test; however, she made an A.

3. Howard is very intelligent, he doesn't believe it.

4. This room doesn't have enough chairs, however it is the only one available.

5. That bedspread is very beautiful; moreover, it is very inexpensive.

6. Gary's girlfriend is very beautiful, she is very rich.

7. Carlos comes from Mexico City, he must know how to speak Spanish.

8. Bill didn't study for the test, therefore he failed it.

9. Carrie is an excellent cook, moreover she makes all of her own clothes.

10. The restaurant is very expensive, the food is excellent.


## EXERCISE 4: GOOD SENTENCES WITH RELATIVE PRONOUNS

The final group of sentence connectors that can be used to combine good sentences in written English are the relative pronouns *who, which,* and *that.* (We have looked at these before, in Chapter 8, Exercise 3.) Consider the following sentences:

Her father grew up in a village. It has only one hundred inhabitants.
Helen is in love with the man. He lives next door.

When these sentences are combined with relative pronouns, the following sentences are created:

Her father grew up in a village which has only one hundred inhabitants.
Her father grew up in a village that has only one hundred inhabitants.

Helen is in love with the man who lives next door.
Helen is in love with the man that lives next door.

Notice that in these sentences commas are not used before the relative pronouns. As you learned in Chapter 8, commas aren't used in these sentences because the relative pronoun does *not* come after the name of a person or a place. However, when the relative pronoun does come after the name of a person or a place, commas are used, as the following sentences illustrate:

Her father grew up in Indian Creek, which has only one hundred inhabitants.
Helen is in love with Raymond Martin, who lives next door.

Now we are ready for the final rule that will help you to distinguish between good sentences and run-ons.

> Rule 16: Relative pronouns (*who, which,* and *that*) are a fourth kind of sentence connector.

> ➤ Proofread the following sentences using Rules 12 and 16, correcting the run-ons with relative pronoun connectors. If a sentence is correct, write "C" after it. The first sentence has been done for you.

1. We found a new ~~apartment, it~~ *apartment that* is very cheap.

2. Anthony bought a camera which was very expensive.

3. Gladys is going out with Dr. Gonzalez, he owns a Mercedes-Benz.

4. They were searching for the dog, it had a broken leg.

5. Bill is dating Gloria Marshall, she has expensive tastes.

6. Robert was cooking a vegetable which Helen didn't like.

7. Joan bought a new sweater, it matches her brown plaid skirt.

8. Joe likes movies which have happy endings.

9. Mark wants to marry a woman who has lots of money.

10. Henry believed the story that you told him.

11. Lisa met a man who had worked at the United Nations.

12. You should never trust anyone who is always cheerful.

## EXERCISE 5: REVIEWING GOOD SENTENCES VERSUS RUN-ONS

Before you do this exercise, review the five rules (Rules 12–16) for recognizing good sentences in written English.

> ➤ Proofread the following sentences. Correct the run-ons with sentence connectors and make sure that commas and semicolons are used correctly.

**Write "C"** after any sentences that are correct. **The first sentence has been done for you.**

1. Susan never waters her plants,ₛₒ they are dying.

2. The television programs last night were terrible, I read a good book.

3. The teachers are on strike, so the mayor is angry.

4. When my parents bought this house, there were no houses close to it.

5. Ray bought a new pair of jeans although he didn't need any.

6. You do this exercise too rapidly, you will make a lot of mistakes.

7. Sue works carelessly, therefore she makes a lot of foolish mistakes.

8. If you quit writing run-on sentences, your grade in English will improve.

9. James Bond entered the room, he saw a beautiful woman.

10. Mark likes shirts which are freshly ironed.

11. I found a stereo system, it costs five hundred dollars.

12. Three basketball players were dropped from the team, their grades were too low.

13. This apartment is very beautiful; however, it is very expensive.

14. The television programs last night were terrible but I watched them anyway.

15. My brother never goes out on dates, he is too shy to talk to a woman.

16. If you read the newspaper every day, your English will improve.

17. David was walking down the street, he heard someone screaming.

18. Ahmad speaks English fluently and he can read French and German.

19. If I have to do one more exercise on run-ons, I will scream.

20. You might as well scream, this is not the last one.

## EXERCISE 6: LONG SENTENCES VERSUS RUN-ONS

In all the examples we have considered so far in the chapter, we examined what happens when two sentences are combined into one sentence. However, it is possible to combine three or four sentences into one sentence. When you do so, you have to be careful to use sentence connectors to link the sentences. In other words, you have to be careful to use sentence connectors to link the *clauses* in the final sentence. (See Chapter 8, Exercise 2 for more discussion of clauses.)

Consider the following examples:

**When you are combining sentences, you need to be careful, you may produce run-on sentences.**

**The television set was broken, so Peter wanted to repair it, he didn't have enough money.**

**José bought a plain hamburger, and Elizabeth bought an Italian beef sandwich, it had green peppers on it.**

All three of these sentences are run-on sentences because they contain three clauses with only one connector. If another connector had been added, the sentences would have been good three-clause sentences. The following examples are good three-clause sentences:

**When you are combining sentences, you need to be careful because you may produce run-on sentences.**

**The television set was broken, so Steve wanted to repair it, but he didn't have enough money.**

**José bought a plain hamburger, and Elizabeth bought an Italian beef sandwich which had green peppers on it.**

It is also possible to produce four-clause sentences like the following ones which have three sentence connectors:

**After David raked the leaves, he wanted to burn them; however, the city has a law against burning leaves, so he put them in the garbage can.**

**It was bright and sunny when we left the city in the morning, but it started to get cloudy before we reached the campground.**

**If you proofread your compositions carefully, your grade in English will improve because you will find your mistakes before your teacher finds them.**

However, if you forget some of the connectors, you may produce run-on sentences like the following ones:

David raked the leaves, he wanted to burn them; however, the city has a law against burning leaves, so he put them in the garbage can.

It was bright and sunny when we left the city in the morning, it started to get cloudy before we reached the campground.

You proofread your compositions carefully, your grade in English will improve, you will find your mistakes before your teacher finds them.

We are now ready for a rule that will help you to distinguish between extra-long good sentences and run-ons.

> *Rule 17:* When you link three clauses, you need to use two connectors to avoid run-on sentences. When you link four clauses, you need to use three connectors to avoid run-on sentences.

➤ Proofread the following examples. Correct the run-ons with sentence connectors, and make sure that commas and semicolons are used correctly. Write "C" after any sentences that are correct. The first sentence has been done for you.

1. Although her mother is opposed to it, Gretchen is dating a ~~man, he~~ *man who* drives a motorcycle.

2. My girlfriend hates football, she loves movies, I love football, I hate movies.

3. If you care for your plants, they will grow, but they will die if you forget about them.

4. Driving a car is very expensive, but no buses run close to my house, I have to drive to school.

5. Greg is a good student who studies four hours every night, Rodney is a poor student who never studies.

6. I'm having a lot of fun; however, I have to get going if I'm going to get up at 4:30 tomorrow.

7. John writes beautiful poetry, he is failing English because he never turns in any compositions.

8. Charlotte is fascinated by people who have emotional troubles, she wants to be a psychiatrist.

9. When we go to the movies, Don cannot enjoy the show unless he has a box of popcorn in his hand.

10. We have worked several exercises on run-ons; however, we still write them; therefore, we need more practice proofreading for run-ons.

## EXERCISE 7: PROOFREADING FOR RUN-ONS

➤ Proofread the following composition, and correct all problems with run-on sentences. The first correction has been made for you.

THE SOAPS

Many people think that soap operas on television are
designed for dumb people, but I disagree. I think that fans of
''the soaps'' must be intelligent because the stories are
very complex. In fact, you want to understand the stories on
soap operas, you must concentrate hard to follow the stories.

First of all, a soap opera fan must learn to recognize
all the characters on the program. This task is not an easy
one, every soap opera has a huge cast of regular characters.
For instance, As the World Turns has thirty characters who
appear regularly, The Guiding Light has twenty-seven regular
characters. When I started watching those soaps, it took me
over a month to get acquainted with all the characters. After
I finally knew all the main characters, I thought that I
could relax, I was wrong. On each program, new characters
would suddenly appear, however I couldn't ignore the new
characters, sometimes they became part of the regular cast.

Although it is hard to get to know all the characters,

it is even harder to get to know all the relationships between all the characters as you can see from the following example. On <u>As the World Turns</u>, there is a woman who is named Lisa, she owns a little boutique. She is the mother of a young lawyer who is called Tom; moreover, she is the ex-wife of a doctor who is named Bob, he is Tom's father. Lisa is also the wife of a lawyer, his name is Grant. He shares an office with Don, who is Bob's brother. Grant was once in love with a woman whose name is Joyce. She later married a lawyer, his name is Don, he shares the office with Grant. Finally, Grant is now married to Lisa, but he thinks that she still loves Bob, the marriage is in trouble. If you think that these relationships are complicated, you should remember that only six characters have been described, but there are thirty characters who appear on the show. As you might expect, those twenty-four other characters have complicated past relationships with each other, moreover they have complicated past or present relationships with the six characters that I discussed in detail.

In conclusion, soap operas are very complex, a dumb person could never understand all the relationships. If you don't believe this, you should find time in your schedule to watch two soap operas that you have never watched before. After you have watched for a week, you will agree with me. To understand soap operas, a person must be intelligent.

## EXERCISE 8: PROOFREADING REVIEW

➤ Proofread the following composition for problems with fragments and run-ons.

## MY APARTMENT

Every now and then, someone asks me. If I like my apartment. I always say that it's not perfect, I don't plan to move, the advantages of my apartment outweigh the disadvantages.

First the disadvantages. One major problem is the landlord. Who resembles Ebenezer Scrooge when it comes to spending money. If there's a problem with the stove or the plumbing, my roommate and I have to complain several times. Before our landlord decides that the problem is really serious. Then he hires the cheapest labor that he can find, so the repair jobs are never done well, in a few weeks, we have the same problem again. The landlord's stingy nature also leads him to set the thermostat at 65 degrees Fahrenheit. To save money on heat. On a cold winter day, when there's not much wind. My roommate and I have to wear heavy sweaters. On windy days, we need to wear long insulated underwear and gloves if we want to stay warm.

The upstairs neighbors are also problems. They have hardwood floors and a dog. Every night at 10:30, they give the dog a half hour of exercise. By throwing a plastic or wooden toy across the floor. The toy and the dog make an incredible racket; however, my roommate and I just tolerate the noise. We complained to the landlord a few times, he didn't do anything about the noise because he's related to the couple upstairs. My roommate and I decided that our lives will be easier. If we just stay up every night until after eleven o'clock although we both have eight o'clock classes three days a week.

In spite of the disadvantages, my roommate and I don't want to move. Because our apartment has some wonderful advantages. For one thing, the rent is very inexpensive. We only pay four hundred dollars a month for a one-bedroom apartment with a living room, kitchen, dining room, and bath. If we moved someplace else. We would have to pay at least five hundred dollars for an apartment of the same size, and we might have to pay six or seven hundred dollars a month.

For a second advantage. The apartment is beautiful. The rooms are big, each room has two large windows that provide lots of light and sunshine to make the place cheerful. The apartment has hardwood floors, they are in perfect condition. The woodwork in the apartment has never been painted, we can still see the natural wood grain on the window frames and the moldings on the walls. There are wonderful views from the west windows. Which look out on a park with lots of trees.

For the last advantage. The location of the apartment is ideal. We live two blocks from school, it only takes us five minutes to walk to class. We're one block away from a grocery store, two blocks from a Laundromat, and two blocks from a pharmacy, so we have all essential services close at hand. Finally, the apartment is one block away from a bus line, we can easily take public transportation. When we want to travel long distances.

In order to have another apartment as good as this one. My roommate and I would have to pay a great deal of money, so we are willing to tolerate the stingy landlord and our noisy upstairs neighbors. The advantages definitely outweigh the disadvantages, we'll stay in this apartment because we know that nothing in life is perfect.

## EXERCISE 9: EXTRA PROOFREADING PRACTICE

➤ Pick one of the pieces you wrote for a journal assignment in Part I of this book. Proofread it, and correct any fragments or run-on sentences you may find.

## EXERCISE 10: PROOFREADING TIP ON WHEN NOT TO USE COMMAS

As you've learned in the exercises you've done so far, you are supposed to use commas with sentence connectors in some places but not in others. In this exercise, we will concentrate on instances where you are *not* supposed to use commas.

Specifically, we will focus on a rule that many experienced writers use: "When in doubt, leave the comma out." What does this rule mean? In simple terms, it means that you use a comma only when you have been taught a rule that tells you to use this punctuation mark.

In this chapter, you've learned four rules that tell you when to use commas—specifically, with comma connectors, two-place connectors, semicolon connectors, and relative pronouns. In Exercise 8 at the end of the last chapter, you learned about using commas with introductory phrases. Review all the rules you've learned. As you do this exercise, and as you proofread all your future work before handing it in, you will be wise to remember *not* to use a comma unless you have learned a rule that tells you to use one.

➤ Proofread the following sentences for problems with commas, adding commas where necessary. Write "C" after any sentences that are correct. The first sentence has been done for you.

1. The man in the plaid shirt is my biology professor.  *C*

2. Karl set the table and Barbara served dinner.

3. The janitor with the tattoo, is named Schneider.

4. After Julie left Max, she realized that she really loved him.

5. The woman with the red hair and the green eyes is my mother-in-law.

6. If you go to Las Vegas you should visit Caesar's Palace.

7. Milton wanted Alice to marry him but he changed his mind when he met her son.

8. Anyone, who enjoys reading, can become a good writer.

9. Alex was tired, so he took a nap.

10. Louise enjoyed her work at the Help Center because she knew that her work made a difference in people's lives.

11. A taxi pulled up in front of the house, and a strange woman stepped from the cab and walked toward the door.

12. Because of the lovely weather Barry and I went for a walk by the lake.

13. All flights have been canceled so my sister will have to stay overnight in Minneapolis.

14. Any student can improve his writing if he is willing to practice.

15. The children playing in the yard are my sister's son and daughter.

# TEN

# PROOFREADING THE SENTENCE: PLURAL MARKERS AND SUBJECT-VERB AGREEMENT

Now that you are familiar with the idea of following rules in order to identify good sentences, you are ready to use the same approach to learn how to proofread your sentences more effectively so that you find any mistakes before your instructor sees your compositions. In this chapter, we will examine some more grammatical rules that you must follow to produce good sentences in written English. As we examine those rules, you will also be given an opportunity to improve your proofreading skills.

## EXERCISE 1: PLURAL MARKERS

Let's begin with a grammatical concept that you already know: *singular and plural nouns.* You are acquainted with three aspects of singular and plural nouns. First, you know that many nouns have both singular and plural forms. For example:

| Singular (one) | Plural (more than one) |
|----------------|------------------------|
| boy            | boys                   |
| girl           | girls                  |
| bus            | buses                  |
| student        | students               |
| college        | colleges               |

Second, you know that most nouns are regular, which means that you add the markers *-s* or *-es* (as in the above examples) to form their plurals. The few nouns that are irregular form their plurals in strange ways. For example:

| **Singular** | **Plural** |
|---|---|
| woman | women |
| man | men |
| child | children |
| tooth | teeth |
| sheep | sheep |

Finally, you know the following rule:

> *Rule 18:* Nouns that name one person or thing should have the singular form, and nouns that name more than one person or thing should have the plural form.

➤ Using Rule 18, proofread the following sentences, and correct any mistakes. If a sentence is correct, write "C" after it. The first sentence has been done for you.

1. Student͜s who study hard will see their grades improve.

2. We saw three men running down the hall.

3. Five security guard are on duty twenty-four hour a day.

4. Too many professors don't care what happens to their student.

5. No class should have more than twenty students.

6. This college is a good school.

7. The only people who should become teachers are those who like child.

8. How many books did you buy?

9. My professor is searching for a rich men to marry.

10. Some people learn from experiences, and some people learn from book.

Most of the words in English that come before nouns—pre-noun words—never change their form from singular to plural when the noun changes, as the following examples show:

| | |
|---|---|
| my brother | my brothers |
| the other student | the other students |
| the blue book | the blue books |
| your teacher | your teachers |

But the form of a few pre-noun words does change when a singular noun becomes plural. Consider the following examples:

| | |
|---|---|
| this boy | these boys |
| that kind | those kinds |
| that student | those students |
| this professor | these professors |

With the pre-noun words *this* and *that,* we always use singular nouns. With *these* and *those,* we always use plural nouns.

> *Rule 19:* The pre-noun words *this* and *that* are used with singular nouns. The pre-noun words *these* and *those* are used with plural nouns.

➤ Using Rule 19, proofread the following sentences, and correct any mistakes. There may be more than one way to correct an error. If a sentence is correct, write "C" after it. The first sentence has been done for you.

11. I like that teacher. *C*

12. Those student never study.

13. My sister doesn't like this kinds of fruit.

14. The students should paint these chairs.

15. All the critics praise that movies.

16. Bill plans to give away these shirt.

17. Those women are intelligent.

18. This class is boring.

19. Nanette doesn't like those kind of men.

20. The words *this* and *these* always confuse that girl.

➤ **Use Rules 18 and 19 to proofread the following paragraph, and correct any mistakes you find.**

My parents refuse to subscribe to cable television because they claim that there are better way to spend our money and time. My father says that cable is more expensive than it's worth. We already get 12 channel on television without paying a penny, but with cable, we would pay fifty dollar a month and just get 28 more channels than we get now. Besides, some of those channel show the same movie over and over and over again, and many of the movie aren't worth seeing once. He says it would be cheaper just to rent those movies that we want to see. My mother thinks my brother and I waste too much time watching television. She claims that we are turning into "couch potato," instead of doing worthwhile thing, like reading book, listening to good music, or going to the health club to get exercise. She thinks that if we had 28 more channel to watch, we would spend the whole day just sitting on the couch, eating potato chip and popcorn, and drinking soft-drinks. In a few month, we would both weigh more than 200 pound. So when other people talk about the game they saw on the sports channel or the story on CNN, my brother and I just sit there like dummy because our parent refuse to spend fifty dollar a month on cable.

# EXERCISE 2: SUBJECT-VERB AGREEMENT WITH PRESENT TENSE VERBS

At some point in your study of English grammar, some teacher may have told you to watch out for mistakes in subject-verb agreement. In this exercise and the next four exercises, we're going to investigate subject-verb agreement in order to help you correct this kind of error when you are proofreading your compositions.

When grammarians talk about subject-verb agreement, they are describing the way in which a particular subject requires a particular verb form. For instance, consider the following sentences:

| | |
|---|---|
| I need more sleep. | I want fried chicken. |
| She needs more sleep. | She wants fried chicken. |
| You need more sleep. | You want fried chicken. |
| He needs more sleep. | He wants fried chicken. |
| We need more sleep. | We want fried chicken. |
| It needs more sleep. | It wants fried chicken. |
| They need more sleep. | They want fried chicken. |

In some of these sentences, the subject forces the writer to use the *-s form* of the verb (*wants, needs*), while in others, the writer has to use the *base form* of the verb, the verb form that has no ending (*want, need*).

In sentences that are used to talk about "present time" (about *now*), the following rule can explain the changes in the verb form:

> **Rule 20:** If the sentence is in present time and the subject of the sentence is *I, you, we,* or *they,* use the base form of the verb. If the subject is *he, she,* or *it,* use the *-s* form of the verb.

➤ Using Rule 20, proofread the following sentences, and correct any mistakes you find. If a sentence is correct, write "C" after it. The first sentence has been done for you.

1. You summarizes the plot.

2. He makes straight A's.

3. We need less work.

4. It seems difficult.

5. He want that pair of jeans.

6. She study four hours every night.

7. I understand this chapter.

8. She knows a great deal about political science.

9. It seem easy.

10. We know this rule.

Although Rule 20 will work for sentences like those which we have discussed so far in this exercise, it cannot account for other kinds of sentences. Consider the following:

Mona needs more sleep.                    Mona wants fried chicken.
The women need more sleep.                The women want fried chicken.
My brother needs more sleep.             My brother wants fried chicken.
The students need more sleep.            The students want fried chicken.
The cat needs more sleep.                 The cat wants fried chicken.
The dogs need more sleep.                 The dogs want fried chicken.

If we want a rule that will help to explain what happens in sentences like these, then we need to add a rule like the following one:

> *Rule 21:* If the sentence is in present time and the subject of the sentence is a singular noun, use the *-s* form of the verb. If the subject of the sentence is a plural noun, use the base form of the verb.

➤ Using Rule 21, proofread the following sentences, and correct any mistakes you find. If a sentence is correct, write "C" after it. The first sentence has been done for you.

11. My sister jog͜s five miles every morning.

12. My brothers clean the garage once a year.

13. Her aunt reads a book a week.

14. Mr. Peppercorn buy three lottery tickets every week.

15. The policeman plans a strike.

16. Our cat chase the neighbor's dog.

17. This book bore me.

18. Judy know a lot about professional football.

19. Our parakeets sleep all day.

20. The boys make too much noise in class.

21. My teacher smoke in class.

22. Mrs. Drummond hates shrimp.

23. The children plays in the alley behind our building.

24. Our church need a new roof.

25. Allen seldom answers the telephone.

The rules we have developed so far will not explain what happens in the following sentences:

He and I need more sleep.
He and she need more sleep.
Jack and Emily want fried chicken.
The dog and cat want fried chicken.

For sentences like these, we need to add the following rule:

*Rule 22:* **In present-time sentences that have *compound subjects* (two nouns or pronouns connected by *and*), use the base form of the verb.**

In addition, the rules we have developed will not explain the following sentences:

I need to sleep.
He needs to sleep.
He and I need to sleep.
He and she need to sleep.

Tom wants to sleep.
Karen wants to sleep.
Tom and Karen want to sleep.

Notice that in sentences like these *sleep* never changes its form. Why? Because *sleep* is not a *real verb*. Sleep is part of the infinitive *to sleep* (part of the *to* form of the verb). Infinitives are *false verbs*, which never change their form to agree with the subject.

---

**Rule 23:** Only *real verbs* show subject-verb agreement.

---

➤ Using Rules 20–23, proofread the following sentences, and correct any mistakes you find. If a sentence is correct, write ''C'' after it. The first sentence has been done for you.

26. Norman enjoy͜s classical music.

27. I prefer to listen to jazz.

28. Khoi and Chang like to play baseball.

29. Paula makes great barbecued ribs.

30. He love to eat Mandarin Chinese food.

31. You notices everything.

32. This city need better public transportation.

33. John likes to visits art museums.

34. Bob and Teddy plays tennis every Saturday.

35. Her three dogs insist on eating steak.

36. He and she teaches school on the West Side.

37. Eggplant gives him indigestion.

38. Mrs. Murphy pretends to enjoys opera.

39. Orange juice contain Vitamin C.

40. Milk provides calcium and Vitamin D.

41. Sonia and Rachel want to become doctors.

42. Rick and Debra gets a balanced diet.

43. German shepherds make great watchdogs.

44. Mike and Cindy likes to play Monopoly.

45. Donald intend to marry Marla.

46. We miss the noise of the big city.

47. The old men plan to attend the meeting.

48. Some students listens carefully in class.

49. Other students never pay attention.

50. That man and his wife looks angry.

## EXERCISE 3: SUBJECT–VERB AGREEMENT WITH HELPING VERBS

The rules we developed in Exercise 2 can also be used to explain how subject–verb agreement works with the verbs *have* and *do,* as the following sentences illustrate:

I have enough food.

Mary has enough food.

John and Mary have enough food.

You have enough food.

I do the dishes every night.

Mary does the dishes every night.

John and Mary do the dishes every night.

You do the dishes every night.

The *-s* form and the base form of the verb are used in exactly those places where our rules say they should be used.

When *have* and *do* are used as helping verbs, they illustrate another fact about subject–verb agreement. Consider the following sentences:

Melissa *has played* the piano for four years.
Melissa and Margaret *have played* the piano for four years.

Karen *does* not *like* heavy-metal records.
Karen *doesn't like* heavy-metal records.

Mark and Karen *do* not *like* heavy-metal records.
Mark and Karen *don't like* heavy-metal records.

*Does* Tom *like* rap music?
*Do* Tom and Karen *like* rap music?

Noticethat when there is a helping verb, *only* the helping verb takes the -*s* form of the verb when it is required; the main verb does not take an -*s* form.

> *Rule 24:* If there is a helping verb, *it alone* must agree with the subject; in such sentences, the main verb does *not* agree.

➤ Using Rules 20–24, proofread the following sentences, and correct any mistakes you find. If a sentence is correct, write "C" after it. The first sentence has been done for you.

1. Joan ~~have~~ has lived in Seattle for three years.

2. Rich and Dorothy do not like poker.

3. He don't study very much.

4. Mr. and Mrs. Siegel travel a lot.

5. Why does women refuse to watch football games?

6. Ed have no common sense.

7. Does the students need more exercise?

8. My sister don't understand men.

9. Has Eliza decided to marry Mr. Higgins?

10. Those men don't appreciate ballet.

11. Karen type very fast.

12. Gentlemen excuse themselves after belching.

13. Where does Marty lives?

14. Ayana likes African restaurants.

15. Do your brother need to learn how to dance?

16. A student sometimes get nervous before a test.

17. My brother and I climb trees a lot.

18. Does John and Frank hate Gordon?

19. Have you heard the news about Suzanne and Lydia?

20. When does the movie begin?

21. The men has been playing checkers for 24 hours.

22. Don't Ken want to buy your car?

23. Mario and Max have all the answers.

24. Do your dogs need a bath?

25. Marcus never underestimate the power of a woman.

For the verb *be,* the rules for subject-verb agreement seem to be much more complex than they are for any other English verb, as the following sentences show:

| | |
|---|---|
| I am happy. | Tom is happy. |
| You are happy. | The teachers are happy. |
| He is happy. | Karen is happy. |
| We are happy. | The students are happy. |
| She is happy. | Tom and Karen are happy. |
| They are happy. | He and she are happy. |
| It is happy. | |

However, if we examine these sentences carefully, we discover that our rules will explain what happens in some of these sentences. If we call *is* the *-s* form of this verb, then all the rules we've used for determining when to use the *-s* form can be used for the verb *be*. So all we need to add is a rule like the following one:

> *Rule 25*: For the verb *be*, when talking about present time, (1) use *is* whenever the rules call for the *-s* form; (2) use *am* if the subject is *I*; (3) use *are* for all the other subjects.

➤ Using Rules 20–25, proofread the following sentences, and correct any mistakes you find. If a sentence is correct, write "C" after it. The first sentence has been done for you.

26. You are easy to please.   *C*

27. Nanette have a new boyfriend.

28. I need a new pen.

29. Tania is polite.

30. He and she is a cute couple.

31. Vicky and Paul is vacationing in San Francisco.

32. Their car needs new tires.

33. Your brother are very handsome.

34. They pretends to be happy.

35. Is Susan and Dennis giving a party?

36. People is tired of violence on television.

37. Bill and Terry have invited us to dinner.

38. Does he know the truth?

39. Laura and Ralph are getting a divorce.

40. We are sleepy.

41. William and Caroline isn't here yet.

42. The children is swinging in the park.

43. You have learned a lot about subject–verb agreement.

44. Sue's brother don't want to get married.

45. I am getting tired of subject–verb agreement exercises.

Finally, we need to consider the nine helping verbs that are sometimes called *modal verbs*. They are: *may, might, can, could, shall, should, will, would, must*. The subject–verb agreement rules for these helping verbs are quite simple. These verbs *never* change form, no matter what the subject of the sentence is, as is shown in the following sentences:

| | |
|---|---|
| I can drive the car. | Tim should study. |
| You can drive the car. | Tim and Clyde should study. |
| Rick can drive the car. | Helen will be there. |
| Debra might drive the car. | Juan and Helen will be there. |

*Rule 26:* The nine modal verbs *never* change their form.

➤ Proofread the following sentences using Rules 24 and 26, and correct any mistakes you find. If a sentence is correct, write "C" after it. The first sentence has been done for you.

46. Vladimir should study more.   *C*

47. Can Anthony see the sign?

48. Tiffany will meets you at the restaurant.

49. It mays rain tomorrow.

50. Must you leave now?

51. Magdalena would likes to meet you.

52. Howard mights get to borrow his father's car.

53. We shall see about that.

54. Could you please be more patient?

55. Where can that boy finds a nurse?

# EXERCISE 4: SUBJECT-VERB AGREEMENT
## WITH COMPOUND VERBS

The examples we have discussed so far have only one verb in a sentence. In this exercise, we will examine what happens when sentences have two or more verbs. Consider the following sentences:

I *sing* and *play* the piano every night.
I *sing, dance,* and *play* the piano every night.
Jim *sings* and *plays* the piano every night.
Jim *sings, dances,* and *plays* the piano every night.

In the first two sentences, the word *I* serves as the subject for *all* the verbs, so all the verbs use the base form. In the last two sentences, the word *Jim* serves as the subject for *all* the verbs, so all the verbs use the *-s* form.

Now consider what happens whenever there is a helping verb in a sentence:

Ken *is singing* and *playing* the guitar.
Ken and Joanie *are singing* and *playing* the guitar.
*Does* Ken *sing* and *play* the piano every night?
*Do* Ken and Joanie *sing, dance,* and *play* the piano every night?

Whenever there is a helping verb, the helping verb is the only one that shows subject–verb agreement.

Therefore, the rules we have used so far can be used in sentences that have compound verbs (two or more verbs) if we add the following rule:

> *Rule 27:* Whenever there is a compound verb, *all verbs* must obey the subject–verb agreement rules.

➤ Using Rules 20–27, proofread the following sentences, and correct any mistakes you find. If a sentence is correct, write "C" after it. The first sentence has been done for you.

1. A good student reads all assignments, take~s~ notes on the assignments, and take~s~ notes in class on lectures.

2. Bob can't walk and chew gum at the same time.

3. Carrie practice the piano in the morning and sing at a nightclub in the evening.

4. Bad drivers runs red lights, passes cars on hills, and speeds around corners.

5. A good teacher prepare for class and grade all assignments quickly.

6. Mrs. Russell wants to see and hear everything in our neighborhood.

7. Ivan eats too little and drink too much.

8. My little brother doesn't smoke or drink.

9. A healthy person eats the right food, sleep eight hours every night, and gets plenty of exercise.

10. Good writers write, rewrite, and proofread.

11. Fragments and run-ons drive me crazy.

12. My little sister ask too many questions and tell too many lies.

13. Can a person love and hates another person at the same time?

14. Has the students finished the assignment and checked all their answers?

15. This restaurant has a pleasant atmosphere and serves good food.

16. A good ball-player should run fast and throws the ball accurately.

17. Does your brother want and needs his wife?

18. My fifteen-month-old brother walks and talks.

19. The churches don't get enough good priests.

20. Do you reads and thinks a lot?

# EXERCISE 5: SPECIAL PROBLEMS
# WITH *HERE* AND *THERE*

In most English sentences, the subject comes *before* the verb, but in some instances, it comes after the verb. Consider the following sentences:

There *is* one problem in this neighborhood.
There *are* several problems in this neighborhood.

Here *is* an example.
Here *are* some examples.

There *seems* to be a misunderstanding.
There *seem* to be some misunderstandings.

From the way the verbs in these sentences change, it is obvious that *here* and *there* are not the subjects of the verbs. In sentences like these, the subject comes *after* the verb. For example:

There *is* one *problem.*
There *are* several *problems.*

Here *is* an *example.*
Here *are* some *examples.*

There *seems* to be a *misunderstanding.*
There *seem* to be some *misunderstandings.*

To determine subject-verb agreement in sentences like these, we need the following rule:

> *Rule 28:* If the sentence begins with *here* or *there,* look *after* the verb to find the subject that will determine the correct verb form.

➤ Proofread the following sentences using Rules 20–28, and correct any mistakes you find. If a sentence is correct, write "C" after it. The first sentence has been done for you.

1. Here comes my brother.   *C*

2. There is fifty cats in the alley behind my house.

3. There are several good reasons for asking your father.

4. There has been too many people sleeping through class.

5. Here are my compositions.

6. There must be two hundred people in this room.

7. Here is the missing books.

8. There seem to be some confusion.

9. There are no explanation for his behavior.

10. There have been three tornado warnings this month.

11. There is some men waiting in the hall.

12. Here is the answer.

13. There is three solutions for this problem.

14. There should be an answer somewhere.

15. Here is her suggestions.

## EXERCISE 6: AGREEMENT WITH VERBS SEPARATED FROM THEIR SUBJECTS

In this exercise, we will consider what happens when a subject and verb are separated by words that fall between them. Let's begin by considering the following sentences:

The girl in the third row *likes* biology.
The girls in the third row *like* biology.
The boy in the blue sweater *lives* on Clark St.
The boy in the blue jeans *lives* on Clark St.

In each of these sentences, a group of words comes between the subject and the verb, but these words have no effect on the verb form, which is determined by the subject. In the first sentence, we use the *-s* form of the verb because the subject of the verb is *the girl*. The girl is the one who "does" the liking. In the second sentence, we use the base form of the verb because the subject of the verb is *the girls*. They are the ones who "do" the liking. So even though the word right in front of the verb (*row*) is singular, the verb will be the base form to agree with the plural subject *the girls*. Similarly, in the third and fourth sentences, the subject is *the boy* because *he* "does" the living. So the verb in both sentences must take the *-s form,* even though in the third, the word right in front of the verb (*sweater*) is singular, and in the fourth, the word right in front of the verb (*jeans*) is plural.

The following rule accounts for sentences like these.

---

*Rule 29:* When a group of words comes between the subject and the verb, those words have no effect on the verb form. The grammatical subject is the word that determines the appropriate form of the verb.

---

➤ Using Rules 20–29, proofread the following sentences, and correct any mistakes you find. If a sentence is correct, write "C" after it. The first sentence has been done for you.

1. The men in the waiting room ~~is~~ *are* Sue's uncles.

2. The woman with the lovely pearl earrings wants to find a matching necklace.

3. Two students in my English class think grammar is fun.

4. The man and woman in the hall wants to speak to the Superintendent of Schools.

5. The child with muddy hands is Sarah's daughter.

6. The children in the park are playing kickball.

7. The dogs in that house is good watchdogs.

8. All the cars in the showroom are on sale for 20 percent off the list price.

9. The oak tree in the park will turn a gorgeous orange after the first frost.

10. The car with the two flat tires needs to be towed.

11. The tomatoes available at the supermarket doesn't taste as good as homegrown ones.

12. The young woman in the green sunglasses don't look interested in meeting you.

## EXERCISE 7: AGREEMENT IN TWO-CLAUSE SENTENCES

In this exercise, we are going to consider what happens when a sentence contains two clauses. (A *clause* is defined as a group of words that has a subject and a verb. If you're not sure how to use this definition, you can look in Chapter 8, Exercise 2, page 141, for a longer discussion of *clauses*.) Let's begin by considering the following sentences:

Juan *loves* Maria, so he and I *plan* to serenade her tomorrow night.
Deanna and Margie *are* going shopping after Deanna *studies* her sociology.

On the basis of sentences like these, we can develop the following rule:

> *Rule 30:* In two-clause sentences, the subject and verb in the first clause agree with one another, and the subject and the verb in the second clause agree with one another.

With sentences like those above, in which two clauses are joined by sentence connectors, it is easy to see how subject-verb agreement works. However, with two-clause sentences that use relative pronouns (the words *who, which,* and *that*), we need to consider how Rule 30 works. Let's consider the following examples first:

My sister *wants* to buy the cabinet which *has* glass doors.
My sister *wants* to buy the cabinets which *have* glass doors.

It's easy to understand why the subject *my sister* requires the verb *wants,* but it may not be so easy to understand why *which* in the first sentence requires *has* and *which* in the second sentence requires *have*. To understand why, we need to discover what the word *which* means in these two sentences. In the first, *which* refers to *the cabinet.* In the second, *which* refers to *the cabinets.* Once we have discovered the meaning of *which* in the two sentences, then we can understand that *which* in the first sentence needs the *-s* form of the verb because *which* refers to a singular noun. We can also see that *which* in the second sentence refers to a plural noun, so it takes the base form of the verb. Using this explanation, we can understand why the verbs in the following sentences take the form they do:

My church *is* looking for a man who *sings* bass.
My church *is* looking for men who *sing* bass.

My sister *wants* to buy the cabinet that *has* glass doors.
My sister *wants* to buy the cabinets that *have* glass doors.

Finally, examine the following sentences:

A man who *has* a bad temper *needs* a patient wife.
Men who *have* bad tempers *need* patient wives.

As soon as we determine what *who* means, it is easy to understand why the first verb in the first of these sentences is *has,* while the first verb in the second is *have.* For the second verb, we need to ask what the subject is. In the first sentence, the subject is *man,* which takes the *-s* form of the verb. In the second, the subject is *men,* so we need the base form of the verb. A similar explanation will work with sentences like the following ones:

A car that *uses* little gas *is* very economical.
Cars that *use* little gas *are* very economical.
A car which *uses* little gas *is* very economical.
Cars which *use* little gas *are* very economical.

➤ Using Rules 20–30, proofread the following sentences, and correct any mistakes you find. If a sentence is correct, write "C" after it. The first sentence has been done for you.

1. Politicians who take bribes make Susan furious.   *C*

2. Ed has no common sense, but his wife love him anyway.

3. A student who don't obey the teachers gets in trouble.

4. My father wants to buy a Mercedes-Benz, but he doesn't have enough money.

5. Lisa knows a man who weigh four hundred pounds.

6. Students often gets nervous when they have to take a test.

7. The women believes that they deserve a night out too.

8. People who read newspapers are well-informed.

9. Although Mark understand his wife, her mother doesn't understand her.

10. A man who knows how to cook will make a good husband.

11. Margaret is looking for a man who have a sense of humor.

12. If your son come to class every day, his grades will improve.

13. I want to buy a shirt which is made of 100 percent cotton.

14. People who eat only junk food might suffers from malnutrition.

15. The students are always complaining about their professors, and the professors is always complaining about their students.

16. We think that this exercise is easy.

17. A dog that barks makes a good watchdog.

18. A woman who is very stubborn need a saintly husband.

19. Because Fred studies a lot, he make straight A's.

20. Anna know that her son is very intelligent.

## EXERCISE 8: PROOFREADING FOR SUBJECT-VERB AGREEMENT AND PLURAL MARKERS

➤ Proofread the following composition, and correct any subject-verb agreement errors and missing plural markers on nouns. The first correction has been made for you.

MY BROTHER AND I

People who meet my brother and me for the first time
thinks we are just friend. It never occurs to anyone that we
could be brothers, much less twin brother. But we are twins,
so perhaps it isn't surprising that even though we are
different in many ways, we are quite similar in a few
important way.

The differences is obvious to anybody who gets to know us. First of all, we don't look at all alike. My brother Juan is six feet tall and weighs 250 pound. I'm five feet ten inches tall and weighs only 190 pounds. Juan have black curly hair, but my hair, which is also curly, is light brown. His complexion is much darker than mine. Some people say we must be lying when we say we are twins because they assumes twins is always identical; however, as my biology textbook point out, some twins are "identical twin," who comes from one fertilized egg, but others is "fraternal twins," who comes from two different egg. As a result, fraternal twins has very different set of chromosomes, so they doesn't look exactly alike. Obviously, my brother and I is fraternal twins. He happen to looks more like our mother, and I look more like our father.

My brother and I not only looks different, but we have very different personality. My brother say he's the strong and silent type. When he meet a girl that he like, he don't know what to say. On the other hand, I am the smooth-talker in the family. When I meet a pretty lady, I am never at a loss for word. Juan doesn't gets angry easily, but when he gets mad, he stay mad for two or three day. I lose my temper easily, but I never stay mad longer than an hours. When someone hurt my feeling, I suffer for a little while, but Juan is really sensitive. When someone hurt his feeling, my brother brood about it for weeks.

But there is more similarities between Juan and me than most people thinks. For one thing, we both loves sports, and we are good athlete, who enjoys football and baseball. In football, Juan plays offensive guard, and I play wide receiver. In baseball, he catch, and I play shortstop.

Because we both want to excel at sports, we has learned
that we must practices discipline in our life. We
runs thirty minute every morning, and we lift weight every
evening. We also study together two or three hour every
evening because we intend to graduate from college and gets
good job.

In addition, Juan and I holds the same basic values. Our
parents are both from Puerto Rico, and they has taught us to
appreciate our Puerto Rican heritage. They want Juan and me
to be fluent bilinguals, so they have encouraged us to
maintain our Spanish as we also learn English. Every Sunday,
our whole family spend time with our grandmother, who don't
speak much English. To communicate easily with her, Juan and
I has to speak Spanish; as a result, we don't have to worry
about forgetting our Spanish. My twin brother and I also is
member of Aspira, which is a club for Puerto Rican young
people. When we attend Aspira meeting, we have an opportunity
to learns more about our people and our culture. Our parents
also wants us to understand how important family
responsibilities is, so when our parents is too busy, my
brother and I sometimes has to go to the doctor with our
grandmother in order to translate what she says into English
and then to translate what the doctor say into Spanish.
Finally, because our parents are Catholics who take their
religion seriously, Juan and I are Catholic who take religion
very seriously. We go to mass each Sunday, and we both has
served as altar boys in our parish.

In conclusion, my brother doesn't looks like me, and his
personality is different from mine. However, when it come to
important things, deep down inside, Juan and I are truly
twins, who shares more than just the same birthday.

# EXERCISE 9: PROOFREADING REVIEW

➤ Proofread the following composition to correct problems with plural markers on nouns, subject-verb agreement, fragments, and run-ons.

## THE BICYCLE SOLUTION

Cars is one of the biggest problem in the United States today. They are responsible for the energy crisis, we wouldn't need as much gasoline. If we didn't have so many car. There is a simple solution to this problem. More people should ride bicycles to school or work, bicycles has many advantage over cars.

Bicycles are much less expensive to own than cars. For one thing, the purchase price of a bike is much cheaper. A bike costs at most a few hundred dollar, a car cost several thousand dollar. Second, a bicycle use no gasoline at all. Something to think about when we have to pay over a dollar for one gallon of gas. Third, the owner of a bicycle don't have to worry so much about the cost of maintenance and repairs. There's only a few parts, they usually don't need more than a little oil and cleaning. Finally, a bicycle rider don't have to spend money on car insurance, state license plates, or a city sticker.

A second advantage is that bicycles contributes to the health of both their owners and the general public. It is easy to see why bicycle owners will become healthier. They will get lots of exercise. Their leg will get strong from pushing the pedals, their lungs and hearts will get strong from working. To pump blood and oxygen to the body. Because the owners get more exercise, they will become healthier. It may not be obvious, but the health of the general public will

improve if more people ride bicycles to work or school. There
are two reason why. First, there will be less air pollution,
bicycles don't give off exhaust fumes, our lungs will get
better. Second, there will be less noise pollution, bicycles
don't make any noise. Our lives will be quieter; therefore,
we won't be so nervous. If people gets less nervous, they
won't have so many headache and stomach ulcers.

Finally, more use of bicycles would make our cities more
pleasant place to live. First of all, people who drives cars
pretends that there are no people in the other cars on the
road, they never smile and wave at their fellow drivers.
Instead, they swear and shake their fists. People who rides
bikes is always smiling and waving at the other people on
bikes and at pedestrians. They even say, ''Hi, how's it
going?'' If more people would ride bikes, people would be
nicer to each other. Second, the cities wouldn't need to
construct so many parking lot, bikes can be stored in very
small spaces. Instead, the city could spend money on more
park with trees, flower, grass, and fountains. Which have
water that gleam in the sunlight. The cities would be more
beautiful, people would be happier. Finally, pedestrians
wouldn't have to fear for their lives. When they cross
the street. A pedestrian has no chance against an
automobile, but bicycles is light in weight, a speeding
bicycle won't kill a pedestrians. The cities would be safer
place to live.

In conclusion. If more people would ride bicycles. Our
world would be much nicer. We would not worry about oil
embargoes, traffic jam, or parking problem. People would have
more money, better health, and a nicer environment. Who could
ask for more?

## EXERCISE 10: EXTRA PROOFREADING PRACTICE

➤ Pick one of the pieces you wrote for a journal assignment in Part I of this book. Proofread it, and correct any problems you may find with: plural markers, subject-verb agreement, fragments, or run-on sentences.

## EXERCISE 11: PROOFREADING TIP ON USING COMMAS WITH COMPOUND CONSTRUCTIONS

In this exercise, we will look at the use of commas with various kinds of compound constructions. In Exercises 2 and 4 in this chapter, you were introduced to compound nouns (nouns joined by *and*) and compound verbs (verbs joined by *and*). Consider the following sentences that contain examples of compound nouns:

Chang-li and Rowena made A's on their compositions.
Diane is going to Los Angeles with Cheryl and Karen.
We toured Arizona and New Mexico on our vacation.

Now examine the following sentences that contain compound verbs:

Saturday is the day when my father shops and cooks.
Sunday afternoon is the time when I read and sleep.
My brother jogs and lifts weights.

Notice that there are no commas before the word *and* in any of these sentences.

Now consider the following sentences that contain what grammarians call a *series* of nouns or verbs—compound constructions made up of three or more nouns or verbs:

Chang-li, Rowena, and Tony made A's on their compositions.
Diane is going to Los Angeles with Cheryl, Karen, and Kathy.
We toured Arizona, New Mexico, Utah, and Colorado on our vacation.
Saturday is the day when my father shops, cooks, cleans, and washes the car.
Sunday afternoon is the time when I read, think, and sleep.
My brother swims, jogs, and lifts weights.

Notice that commas are placed between the nouns in the series and before the word *and*.

From the examples above, you can conclude that when you put two words together in a compound construction, you don't use a comma to separate the items. However, when you put three or more items together to form a series, you do use commas to separate them.

So far we have only considered compound constructions that contain nouns or verbs, but there are other kinds of compound constructions. Consider the following sentences, which contain compound phrases:

> Melinda enjoys listening to records and watching movies.
> Melinda enjoys listening to records, watching movies, and playing the piano.

> Steve dropped the bag of groceries and ran into the street.
> Steve dropped the bag of groceries, ran into the street, and pulled the child to safety.

> Secretaries are expected to type letters and take shorthand.
> Secretaries are expected to type letters, take shorthand, and answer the phone for the boss.

Again, no commas are used with compound constructions of two phrases, but commas are used to separate the members of a series of three or more phrases.

To summarize what you've learned in this exercise, use the following rule:

> *Rule 31:* Whenever you have a compound construction of two words or phrases, don't use a comma before *and*. Whenever you have a series of three or more words or phrases, use commas to separate all the members of the series.

➤ Using Rule 31, proofread the following sentences, and correct any mistakes you find. If a sentence is correct, write "C" after it. The first sentence has been done for you.

1. While Ruth and Connie were in Chicago, they visited the Sears Tower, the Art Institute, and the Museum of Science and Industry. *C*

2. Kenneth won't eat broccoli cauliflower and brussels sprouts.

3. The President, the Secretary of State, and the Secretary of Defense tried to negotiate between the Soviet Union and Latvia.

4. Margaret sings dances, and plays the guitar.

5. Barney entered the building, punched the time clock, and went to his desk.

6. Rebecca has had measles mumps and chicken pox.

7. Tom fixed dinner for Jeanette, Melissa, and Stephen.

8. Shannon and Donna left the cabin walked to the beach and searched for seashells.

9. One-year-old Corey took four steps smiled at his mother, and dove into his father's arms.

10. Teresa borrowed money from my sister her sister and your sister.

11. Tatiana studied German, French, and English.

12. Brian mowed the lawn and washed the car.

# ELEVEN

## PROOFREADING THE SENTENCE: PAST TENSE AND PAST PARTICIPLE MARKERS

As you learned in Chapter 10, when you proofread compositions, you need to pay attention to the ends of words to make sure that you mark necessary word endings, like plural markers or subject-verb agreement markers. In this chapter, we will consider some other *word-end markers* that you should keep in mind when you proofread compositions.

### EXERCISE 1: SIMPLE PAST TENSE AND REGULAR VERBS

When you write about events that occurred in the past, you must make sure that all the verbs are marked with the *past tense form* of the verb. What is the *past tense form*? For most English verbs, it is the *-ed* form. The following sentences illustrate this:

I *attended* the lecture last night.
Lucy *walked* to school yesterday.
Dale *joined* the club last Thursday.
We *played* tennis Saturday.
Jack and Emily *invited* Ed and Sue to the party.

Notice that the past tense form of the verb ends in *-ed* no matter what the subject of the verb is. So, for this verb form, you don't have to worry about subject-verb agreement.

> **Rule 32:** Verbs that name events that happened in the past should be in the past tense form of the verb—the *-ed* form for most verbs.

➤ Using Rule 32, proofread the following sentences and correct any past-tense problems. Write "C" after any sentences that are correct. The first sentence has been done for you.

1. The boy climb~ed~ through the window last night.

2. Ruth needed a new coat.

3. The students listen attentively to the lecture.

4. The elderly woman dropped her shopping bag.

5. My sister wanted a boy, but her husband want a girl.

6. The professor liked my idea for a paper.

7. Don jump the fence.

8. Rhett Butler laughed at Scarlett and walk out the door.

9. Marvin dropped the class before he attend it.

10. The teacher ask for our attention.

11. Jennifer always looked stupid.

12. The assignment seem easy.

13. The roof of the garage collapsed.

14. Nancy's brother played center for the Minnesota Vikings.

15. Jerry enjoy Emily's predicament.

16. They turned the key, open the door, and walk into the room.

17. General Custer and his men wait for the Indians.

18. We avoided the topic of abortion.

19. Mr. Chang noticed the crack in the window.

20. The students applaud the professor for two minutes.

Some sentences seem to be exceptions to Rule 32:

Diana *wanted to attend* the concert.
Miguel *hoped to visit* the Statue of Liberty.
We *invited* them *to join* us.

Why is there no past tense ending on *attend, visit,* and *join*? Because *attend, visit,* and *join* are not real verbs. They are parts of *false verbs,* as we discussed in Chapter 8, Exercise 4 (see page 145)—parts of infinitives or *to* forms of the verbs.
To explain sentences like these, we need to add the following rule:

> *Rule 33:* Only real verbs are marked for past tense.  *False verbs* are never marked for past tense.

➤ Using Rules 32 and 33, proofread the following sentences, and correct any problems with tense. If a sentence is correct, write "C" after it. The first sentence has been done for you.

21. The teacher seemed to believe my story. *C*

22. The reporter wanted to learned the truth.

23. Gail and Jessica try to explain their problem.

24. In 1492, Columbus sail the ocean blue.

25. Queen Isabella expected him to discover gold.

26. The students decide to talk to the Dean.

27. The Senate voted to approved the bill on the budget, but the House refuse.

28. The South attempted to secede from the Union.

29. The women refused to listened to Phyllis.

30. The professor intended to grade the papers, but he played tennis instead.

31. Iraq invaded Kuwait in the summer of 1990.

32. Mark learn to cook when his wife start college.

33. Mrs. Stephens promised to visit my aunt.

34. The men offered to washed the windows.

35. Emma managed to pass the course.

## EXERCISE 2: THE VERB *DO* AND THE PAST TENSE

Whenever you use the verb *do* in the past tense, you need to keep two things in mind. First, you need to remember that *do* is an irregular verb that forms its past tense in an unusual way. The following sentences illustrate this:

Mark *did* the dishes last night.
The class *did* this exercise last week.

Second, you need to be aware of what happens when the past tense form *did* is used as a helping verb. Examine the following sentences:

Maureen *did* not *invite* Natalie to the wedding.
Debbie and Marit *did* not *play* handball on Saturday.
*Did* Anna *walk* to school yesterday?
*Did* the students *attend* the lecture?

To understand what happens in these sentences, we need to use the following rule:

> *Rule 34:* When *did* is used as a helping verb, the main verb does not have a past tense ending. The main verb uses the base form of the verb.

➤ Proofread the following sentences using Rule 34, and correct any problems
with tense. If a sentence is correct, write "C" after it. The first sentence
has been done for you.

1. Did the Senator cheated on his taxes?

2. My grandfather did not appreciate the joke.

3. Where did the president move?

4. My brother did not learned the lesson which my father want him to
learned.

5. Why did the chicken crossed the road?

6. Did the flood water reach your house?

7. Didn't you visited the Washington Monument?

8. When did the Governor arrive?

9. Did the thunderstorm disturbed your sleep?

10. The gun slip from my hand.

11. Mr. Doolittle didn't want to listened to his wife.

12. The business did not need a loan.

13. How did Serena pass the test when she didn't study for it?

14. My sisters did not enjoy the sermon.

15. Did you finished the exercise?

## EXERCISE 3: THE VERB *BE* AND THE PAST TENSE

For almost all English verbs, you never have to worry about subject-verb
agreement with past tense forms. However, there is one verb that does force you
to worry about subject-verb agreement: it is the verb *be*. Consider the following
sentences:

I *was* sick yesterday.        We *were* sick yesterday.
You *were* sick yesterday.     She *was* sick yesterday.
He *was* sick yesterday.       They *were* sick yesterday.
It *was* sick yesterday.

To explain sentences like these, we need the following rule:

> *Rule 35:* For past tense forms of the verb *be:* (1) use *was* if the
> subject is *I, he, she,* or *it;* (2) use *were* if the subject is *you,*
> *we,* or *they.*

➤ Proofread the following sentences using Rule 35, and correct any mistakes.
If a sentence is correct, write "C" after it. The first sentence has been done
for you.

1. We ~~was~~ *were* disappointed.

2. He was handsome.

3. It was necessary.

4. I were in the library.

5. You were a great athlete in your youth.

6. They were unbelievable.

7. I was on time.

8. You were terrific.

9. She were pretty.

10. They was very tired.

11. We were the best team in the tournament.

12. Where was she?

Rule 35 does not explain what happens in the following sentences:

My brother *was* sick yesterday.
My brothers *were* sick yesterday.

Dale *was* sick yesterday.
Anne and Dale *were* sick yesterday.

For sentences like these, we need to add the following rule:

> *Rule 36:* **For the past tense of** *be,* **if the subject is a singular noun, use** *was;* **if the subject is a plural noun or a compound noun (two or more nouns or pronouns connected by** *and),* **use** *were.*

➤ Using Rules 35 and 36, proofread the following sentences, and correct any mistakes. If a sentence is correct, write "C" after it. The first sentence has been done for you.

13. The men ~~was~~ *were* waiting in the kitchen.

14. The priests were unhappy with the archbishop.

15. Dr. Herman was lecturing on Irish literature.

16. The tango and the jitterbug was popular dances in the 1940s.

17. The monkey was chattering at the people.

18. The witnesses was questioned by the police.

19. Alderman Gutierrez was a student here in the 1970s.

20. Barbara and I was in support of the strike.

21. The people was complaining about the public school system.

22. The segregation laws was declared unconstitutional.

23. President Lincoln and President Kennedy were both assassinated.

24. We was discovering the truth about South Africa.

25. The children were very tired.

26. Carrie and Frank were late for the party.

27. You was laughing while we was singing.

Finally, we need to consider sentences like the following ones:

There *was* a problem in the city.
There *were* three problems in the city.

There *was* a misunderstanding.
There *were* some misunderstandings.

For sentences that begin with *there,* the real subject of the verb always comes *after* the verb. (See Chapter 10, Exercise 5, page 186, for a longer discussion of sentences like these.)

> *Rule 37:* If the sentence begins with *there,* look after the verb to find the subject in order to discover what past tense form of *be* to use.

➤ Using Rules 35–37, proofread the following sentences, and correct any mistakes. If a sentence is correct, write "C" after it. The first sentence has been done for you.

28. There were four kinds of cake at the bazaar.  *C*

29. There was a fly in my soup.

30. There were no reason for him to leave.

31. There was seven women in my auto mechanics class.

32. There was some students and a faculty member playing pool in the recreation room.

33. There was a man hiding in the hallway.

34. There were some people who disliked Reagan.

35. There were one good dancer in the company.

36. There was three paintings which I wanted to buy.

37. There wasn't any fire fighters on duty at my station during the strike.

## EXERCISE 4: PAST TENSE FORMS OF SOME COMMON IRREGULAR VERBS

If you assume that most verbs in English form their past tense by using the *-ed* form of the verb, you will be right most of the time. However, as you already know, some verbs form their past tense in strange and peculiar ways. They are the irregular verbs. For these verbs, you must simply memorize the correct past tense forms.

In this exercise, you will work on thirty-five of the common irregular verbs. You should make sure now that you know how to use these verbs in the past tense. Then, as you continue to develop your writing skills in other courses, you can add other irregular verbs to the list.

### Irregular Verbs: List 1

| Base Form | Past Tense Form |
|-----------|-----------------|
| begin | began |
| break | broke |
| bring | brought |
| build | built |
| choose | chose |
| come | came |
| eat | ate |
| fall | fell |
| feel | felt |
| find | found |
| forget | forgot |

➤ Review Rules 32–34. Then proofread the following sentences, correcting any mistakes you find. If a sentence is correct, write "C" after it. The first sentence has been done for you.

1. Did they ~~began~~ begin to study irregular verbs?

2. Susan and Paul felt foolish.

3. My brother-in-law find a diamond necklace on the sidewalk.

4. Nathan Hale was forced to choose between liberty and death.

5. When Adam and Eve eat the apple, they fell from grace to sin.

6. How did you break your leg?

7. Walter did not find a taxi.

8. We come to class every day last term.

9. I forget to bring the ice.

10. Noah built a huge boat.

11. Did the professor and her husband brought the records?

12. Bob and Melanie did not feel tired.

13. Where did they found this book?

14. Bill choose to eat the whole pizza.

15. Did the president come to the meeting?

16. Khoi Nguyen brought a delicious Vietnamese rice dish to the party.

17. The class decided to built a model of Shakespeare's Globe Theatre.

18. George broke the window.

19. Why did you ate the whole pie?

20. When Norma began to fall, she grabbed my arm.

21. Why did you forgot your driver's license?

22. Did you find my letter?

23. Eduardo began to build a coalition of student groups.

24. My brother feel depressed after the class.

25. Raymond never forgot where he come from.

## Irregular Verbs: List 2

| Base Form | Past Tense Form |
| --- | --- |
| give | gave |
| go | went |
| grow | grew |
| have | had |
| hear | heard |
| keep | kept |
| know | knew |
| leave | left |
| make | made |
| mean | meant |
| meet | met |
| put | put |

➤ Proofread and correct the following sentences, just as you did the previous set.

26. Mario know every answer on the test.

27. Did Gunter keep trying to make a perfect score?

28. Pete did not had a headache.

29. I heard this joke before.

30. Where did you put the paper?

31. The teacher give Miranda a D on her paper.

32. My doctor leave the office to go to the hospital.

33. I meant for you to heard that.

34. The plants grew very quickly.

35. The priest and the minister meet Mrs. McKinney as she left the room.

36. Valerie keep a journal last winter.

37. François wanted to went to Los Angeles.

38. Did you mean to have a nervous breakdown?

39. Why did the teacher give this assignment?

40. My aunt and uncle did not put their money in the bank; instead, they kept it under their mattress.

41. We finally meet his parents last night.

42. The judge knew the truth before you made your statement.

43. Sandy's uncle growed tomatoes last summer.

44. How often did they gave money to the church?

45. Elizabeth have the flu last week.

46. We maked this vase for you.

47. Did you know the right answer?

48. Why didn't Harry leave the party before midnight?

49. When did Myrna made her decision?

50. We hear him talking, but we didn't believe him.

## Irregular Verbs: List 3

| Base Form | Past Tense Form |
| --- | --- |
| read | read |
| run | ran |
| say | said |
| see | saw |
| seek | sought |
| speak | spoke |
| take | took |
| teach | taught |
| tell | told |

## *Irregular Verbs: List 3* (cont'd)

| Base Form | Past Tense Form |
|---|---|
| think | thought |
| understand | understood |
| write | wrote |

Proofread and correct the following sentences just as you did the previous two sets.

51. Did she told the truth?

52. The men spoke to you about this before.

53. Susan and Irma take General Biology last year.

54. Did the students thought that the teacher say to write a composition?

55. Where did you read this?

56. Plato always seek the truth.

57. Paul ran the mile in four minutes.

58. The professor taught us to ask questions when we did not understand what she say.

59. Noriko saw the accident.

60. Linda read the composition which Sheila write.

61. Dorothy never understood one word which James said.

62. Mr. Douglas wanted to ran for President.

63. Why did you seek to understand the universe?

64. Did you saw Spike Lee's new movie?

65. Did the mayor speak to Mr. Camacho before she nominated him for the School Board?

66. Your counselor told you not to take Popular Culture.

67. Our history professor did not taught us about World War II.

68. I thought I saw O. J. Simpson at the mall.

69. Did the police officer agree to take this test?

70. You tell me once, but I forgot.

71. Francesca wrote a composition on the story which you tell her.

72. No one understood the professor's lecture.

73. His sister thought that he took his medicine every morning.

74. Where did you saw this man?

75. My senator said that the president understood our state's economic problems.

## EXERCISE 5: PROBLEMS WITH TENSE AGREEMENT

In Chapter 10, you learned about one kind of agreement problem that you encounter when you are proofreading compositions—subject-verb agreement. In this exercise, we will consider another kind of agreement problem that you have to worry about when you are proofreading—*tense agreement*.

What is tense agreement? In simple terms, it means that when you start with a particular verb tense in a sentence, all the verbs in the sentence *usually* have the same tense. Consider the following sentences, all of which use past tense verb forms:

> After Bill *washed* the car, he *waxed* it.
> Sue *wrote* her composition before she *went* home.
> Bill *cooked* dinner, and Helen *took* a nap.
> While Bill *studied* his English, Jane *worked* on her chemistry, and
>    Greta *did* her calculus assignment.

Now consider the following sentences, all of which use present tense verb forms:

> When Bill *takes* the bus to school, he *leaves* home an hour earlier than usual.
> After Margaret *washes* the car, she always *waxes* it.
> Stacy *enjoys* soccer, but Della *prefers* football.

> When students *write* compositions, they *get* better grades if they *proofread* their compositions carefully.

In all the above sentences, the writer started with one verb tense and continued to use that tense throughout the sentence.

If you were reading very carefully, you noticed that when we defined tense agreement above, we used the word *usually*. This word suggests that writers sometimes change tenses in the middle of a sentence. In general, a writer makes a change in tense if the two parts of the sentence occurred at different times. For instance, consider the following sentences:

> When I *was* a child, I *enjoyed* climbing trees, but I *don't enjoy* that activity now.
> Bill *played* tennis when he *was* a teenager, but now he *plays* golf.
> Maria *had* blond hair when she *was* little, but now she *has* brown hair.
> Men once *preferred* wives who *stayed* home and *took* care of the house, but now men *prefer* wives who *work* and *help* bring home money.

In these four sentences, the writer uses the past tense when he or she is discussing something that was true in the past, but then shifts to the present tense to indicate that he or she is now discussing something that is true at the present time.

All of these sentences illustrate the rule for tense agreement, which can be summarized as follows:

> *Rule 38:* All verbs in a sentence should be in the same tense *if* all the events in the sentence happened at the same time. If the events in the sentence happened at different times, then the writer changes tense in order to show that different times are being discussed.

> Use Rule 38 to proofread the following sentences, correcting any problems with tense. If a sentence is correct, write "C" after it. The first sentence has been done for you.

> 1. Marcus talked to the doctor while his father waited in the hall.   *C*

> 2. I told him what I knew, and he becomes angry.

> 3. David speaks Italian, and he reads French.

4. Carl asked Elizabeth to marry him, but she refused.

5. Mark entered the house, and he hears a noise.

6. Tom and Karen left the house and walk to the car.

7. Dmitri borrowed Kathy's car, and he dents the fender.

8. After Anastasia finishes her assignments, she practices the guitar for an hour before she goes to bed.

9. Steve wrote a letter to the President, but he never received an answer.

10. Sofia started to cry when she learned that she was the winner of the contest.

11. My brother was at the airport when someone calls his name on the loudspeaker.

12. When the movie ended, Philip jumps up and cheers.

13. The principal walked into the room and congratulates the students on their test scores.

14. Now that I understand verb tenses, I feel more confident when I proofread.

15. I hope the day comes when I no longer have to worry about verbs.

16. When we were children, we thought that adults knew everything, but now as adults, we understand that we do not know everything.

17. As a boy, I enjoy fishing, but now as an adult, I think that fishing is boring.

18. Then her hair was curly, but now it was straight.

19. When she was a child, Janice is afraid of the dark, but now she is afraid of nothing.

20. My brother wrote poetry when he was a child, but now he refuses to write anything, so he is failing Writing 101.

## EXERCISE 6: THE PAST PARTICIPLE: THE HELPING VERB *HAVE* AND THE *-ED* VERB FORM

In Exercise 1, you learned that the *-ed* verb form is used to mark verbs as past tense. In this exercise and the next one we will consider two other uses of the *-ed* verb form.

Let's begin by considering the following sentences:

I *have lived* in the same apartment for five years.
Greg *has lived* in the same apartment for five years.
Marsha *has played* the piano for eight years.
Pablo and Javad *have attended* every class.

These sentences show that whenever you use the helping verb *have,* you must use the *-ed* form for all regular verbs. Because most grammar books call this construction "*have* plus the past participle verb form," we will call this particular use of the *-ed* form the *past participle form.* So, to account for sentences like those above, we are going to use the following rule:

> *Rule 39:* Whenever the helping verb *have* is used, the past participle form of the main verb should be used. (For most verbs, the past participle form of the verb is the *-ed* form.)

➤ Proofread and correct the following sentences, using Rule 39. If a sentence is correct, write "C" after it. The first sentence has been done for you.

1. Marlene and Michael have ask~ed~ me to serve as best man at their wedding.

2. Ryne Sandberg has played with the Chicago Cubs for several years.

3. The teachers have picketed the public schools for two weeks.

4. The terrorists had bomb three embassies that month.

5. Gretchen has study Spanish for three years.

6. That volcano has erupted three times this year.

7. Tornadoes had destroy several cities in the Midwest.

8. Scientists have discover a cure for cancer.

9. Sergeant Okano has stayed in Hawaii for seven weeks.

10. The travel agent had arrange a trip to Buenos Aires for us.

11. Father Price has attended every lecture this term.

12. Cheryl has live in Dallas for three years.

13. Don has studied Medieval philosophy for thirteen years.

14. The city's problems have increase in the past two years.

15. The school had need a new curriculum for many years.

16. Have the students finish the test?

17. Has your father noticed your new haircut?

18. The price of pork had not increase.

19. Josephine has already walked the dog.

20. Mrs. Dawson had never taste fajitas.

## EXERCISE 7: THE PAST PARTICIPLE: THE HELPING VERB *BE* AND THE *-ED* VERB FORM

There is another construction in which the *-ed* form of the verb is used. To understand this use of the *-ed* form, we will begin by considering the following sentences that use simple past tense forms:

Three hundred students *attended* the lecture.
Five detectives *chased* the thief.
A tornado *destroyed* the garage.

For each of these sentences, there is another sentence which means the same thing:

The lecture *was attended* by three hundred students.
The thief *was chased* by five detectives.
The garage *was destroyed* by a tornado.

The verbs in the first group of sentences are called *active verbs* because the subject of the verb actively *performs* the action of the verb: The students *do* the attending; the detectives *do* the chasing; the tornado *does* the destroying. On the other hand, the verbs in the second group of sentences are called *passive verbs* because the subject of the verb does *not* actively perform the action of the verb: The lecture does not attend; the thief does not chase; the garage does not destroy. Instead, someone else or something else performs the action; someone else or something else *does* something to the subject, which is *passive* (not active).

Given below are some more examples of active verb forms (in which the subject performs the action) and passive verb forms (in which the subject does not perform the action):

A justice of the peace *married* Lily and George.
Lily and George *were married* by a justice of the peace.

An old man *frightened* the boys.
The boys *were frightened* by an old man.

Marie Curie *discovered* radium.
Radium *was discovered* by Marie Curie.

The passive verb sentences we have examined so far have three things in common: (1) The subject does not perform the action. (2) The verb has a form of *be* and the past participle form of the verb (the *-ed* form for most verbs). (3) At the end of the sentence, there is a phrase beginning with *by* that tells who or what performed the action.

Not all sentences with passive verb forms contain a phrase beginning with *by*. Consider the following sentences:

Martina *was invited* to the party.
The fender of my car *was dented*.
Steve and Edith *were married* on June 3.
The theft *was reported* at 5:00 A.M.
Bob's car *is parked* in the alley.
Racquetball *is played* indoors.
Students *are asked* not to smoke in class.
Seniors *are allowed* to register first.

In these sentences, we are not told *who* or *what* performed the action. However, these sentences are similar to other passive verb sentences in two ways: (1) The subject of the verb does not perform the action. (2) The verb has a form of *be* and the past participle form of the verb.

To explain what happens to the verb in all the passive verb sentences we have examined in this exercise, we need the following rule:

> *Rule 40:* In sentences with passive verb forms, use a form of *be* and the past participle form of the main verb (the *-ed* form for most verbs).

➤ Using Rule 40, proofread and correct the following sentences. If a sentence is correct, write "C" after it. The first sentence has been done for you.

1. In 1849, gold was discover*ed* in California.

2. The runways were covered by ash from the volcano.

3. The witnesses were question by the police.

4. The ball was dropped by the catcher.

5. Students are require to take a competence test.

6. The Confederate army was defeat at Gettysburg.

7. The class was bore by the guest lecturer.

8. Was the garage destroy by a tornado?

9. Five hundred cars are parked in the lot.

10. Glenn was congratulated by the principal.

11. When was the Salt II Treaty signed?

12. The students were not amuse by the professor's joke.

13. The President is please by the results of the election.

14. This play was never performed on Broadway.

15. The sentences were dictate by a substitute teacher.

16. Where were the terrorists discover?

17. The plan was approved by the committee.

18. Mr. Winters was treated by the best doctors in the city.

19. The students are test on their language skills at the beginning of each term.

20. Crime was considered the number one problem in the United States in 1990.

## EXERCISE 8: PAST PARTICIPLES FOR SOME COMMON IRREGULAR VERBS

If you assume that most verbs in English form their past participles by using the *-ed* form of the verb, you will be right most of the time. However, with irregular verbs like those we discussed in Exercise 4 (see page 208), you will have to memorize the past participle forms that should be used with the helping verb *have* and with passive verb forms.

In this exercise we will concentrate on the verbs we considered in Exercise 4 as well as two other irregular verbs: *be* and *do*.

### Irregular Verbs: List 1

| Base Form | Past Tense | Past Participle |
|-----------|------------|-----------------|
| be | was or were | been |
| begin | began | begun |
| break | broke | broken |
| bring | brought | brought |
| build | built | built |
| choose | chose | chosen |
| come | came | come |
| do | did | done |
| eat | ate | eaten |
| fall | fell | fallen |
| feel | felt | felt |
| find | found | found |
| forget | forgot | forgotten |

➤ Review Rules 39 and 40. Then proofread the following sentences, and correct any problems with past participle verb forms. If a sentence is correct, write "C" after it. The first sentence has been done for you.

1. The professor has ~~being~~ *been* sick for two weeks.

2. The Sears Tower was built in the early 1970s.

3. I have already forget the rules for subject-verb agreement.

4. The curfew laws were broken by the students.

5. We had begun a long struggle.

6. Your brother has fell in love.

7. The missing money was found in the garage.

8. The years have bringed Cheryl and Diane closer together.

9. The day of judgment had came.

10. The girls have done their homework.

11. The school board had chose a new principal.

12. The rabbits have ate all our lettuce.

13. Have they felt happy all week?

14. Where have you been?

15. Mr. Wang had broke his arm.

16. Has Dr. Allison find the chalk?

17. My composition was eaten by my dog.

18. Four students were chosen to serve on the committee.

19. The rules have begun to change.

20. Was this cake brought by Mrs. Bridges?

21. Tony has did all the work for the committee.

22. A total of 100,000 immigrants had come to the United States from Cuba in one month.

23. Nancy and Elizabeth have build a treehouse.

24. Steve had forgotten his pen again.

25. Jeffrey has feel foolish for two weeks because he has fallen in love with a picture of a woman in the newspaper.

### Irregular Verbs: List 2

| Base Form | Past Tense | Past Participle |
|-----------|-----------|-----------------|
| give | gave | given |
| go | went | gone |
| grow | grew | grown |
| have | had | had |
| hear | heard | heard |
| keep | kept | kept |
| know | knew | known |
| leave | left | left |
| make | made | made |
| mean | meant | meant |
| meet | met | met |
| put | put | put |

➤ Using Rules 39 and 40, proofread and correct the following sentences, as you did the previous set.

26. The students were given fifteen minutes to finish the quiz.

27. The mayor has known my father for ten years.

28. We had heard that story before.

29. This dress was make for you.

30. Her teenage son has grew six inches this year.

31. Professor McQueen has went crazy.

32. Rita has had a cold for a month.

33. The class had not meet for a week.

34. The books were putted in the filing cabinet.

35. Were the letters left on the desk?

36. Gary has not have time to call you this week.

37. Were the people kept in ignorance by the dictator?

38. At last, John's voice was heard by the instructor.

39. My aunt was met at the airport by my father.

40. Corn was first grown by Native Americans.

41. John and Sherry were mean for each other.

42. You have already made too many mistakes in your life.

43. The Senator had keep his promises to the voters.

44. The children have put the flowers on the altar.

45. Has William gone to Puerto Rico?

46. Has the President leave the White House?

47. Jerry had knew the truth for two weeks.

48. The Dean had given the students an ultimatum.

49. Where have the years went?

50. My neighbors have had a lot of trouble with their daughter.

## Irregular Verbs: List 3

| Base Form | Past Tense | Past Participle |
| --- | --- | --- |
| read | read | read |
| run | ran | run |
| say | said | said |
| see | saw | seen |
| seek | sought | sought |

## Irregular Verbs: List 3 (cont'd)

| Base Form | Past Tense | Past Participle |
|---|---|---|
| speak | spoke | spoken |
| take | took | taken |
| teach | taught | taught |
| tell | told | told |
| think | thought | thought |
| understand | understood | understood |
| write | wrote | written |

➤ Using Rules 39 and 40, proofread and correct the following sentences, as you did the previous set.

51. Had he tell you the truth?

52. Poets have wrote about the beauty of nature.

53. The hostages were taken to the airport.

54. The race was run in one minute fifty seconds.

55. José has read the entire *Encyclopedia Britannica*.

56. We were taught the rules for past participles.

57. The professor had spoke to Bonnie about her absences.

58. Have you understand all the things which he has said?

59. Wanda has always sought the truth.

60. The suspect was seen at the corner of Belmont and Clark.

61. Have you ever think about becoming a doctor?

62. This novel was written in 1985.

63. This teacher has taught us nothing.

64. Where had the security guards took him?

65. The book was readed by every student in class.

66. No words were spoken.

67. When were you told about the plan?

68. Mark and Sandy had saw the light.

69. My mother has always understood me.

70. Why had she seek to deceive him?

71. Mr. Burke has run for President three times.

72. I have always thought that you were taught to tell the truth.

73. What was say about me at the meeting?

74. Have you written your composition?

75. What have you heard?

## EXERCISE 9: PROOFREADING FOR PAST TENSE AND PAST PARTICIPLE MARKERS

➤ Proofread the following composition, and correct problems with past tense and past participle markers. The first correction has been made for you.

AN EXPERIENCE THAT CHANGED MY LIFE

When I was in elementary school, my best friend Mary and I ~~was~~ were the only girls in our neighborhood, but there was lots of boys. At first, we pretend that the boys did not existed. We only did the things which little girls were supposed to do. We played house, and we try to be like our mothers. We dress up in our mothers' clothes, jewelry, and makeup, and we pretend to cook meals on our toy stoves. We changed the diapers on our dolls, and we give tea parties for one another with toy cups which were fill with Kool-aid.

But then one day Mary and I have an argument over some silly subject which I have forgot, and we didn't spoke to one another for a week. During that week, I discovered that I have no one to play with. Because I was lonesome, I ask the boys to let me play cops and robbers with them. They give me a funny look, but they agreed to let me play. The robbers chose me to be on their side even though they did not thought that I was able to run fast enough to get away from the cops. They were surprise when they learn that I ran as fast as they do. I was surprise too, but for a different reason. I realized that I really enjoy the game which Mary and I had always call a stupid game.

From that moment on, I was a "tomboy," a girl who liked to play boys' games, and my friend Mary become one too as soon as she and I decide to be friends again. We played cowboys and Indians. We play cops and robbers. We even learn to play baseball. We become good enough at baseball that the boys was happy to have us on their team.

That experience change my life, because as I have grew older, I have discover the advantages of being a tomboy. For one thing, we tomboys learned to respected our own abilities. We learn that we was able to competed with boys, so we feel that we were equal to boys. We saw no reason why we had to grew up to be only wives and mothers. We assume that we could also have jobs if we wanted to. In addition, we tomboys learned to respect boys' abilities and interests. We know how hard it was to throw a baseball well, so we respected boys for being good at baseball. We also came to understood why boys liked sports so much. As a result, when we grew older, we were able to share things with our boyfriends that other girls only pretended to shared. We really enjoy watching football games with our boyfriends. We really cared about the pennant race in baseball, so we did not minded when our boyfriends talk all the time about baseball. Because we respected boys' abilities and interests, we had good friendships with men.

As it turned out, I was really lucky that I have that argument with Mary. I did not lose her friendship. Instead, I gained a great deal when I was introduce to the life of a tomboy.

## EXERCISE 10: PROOFREADING REVIEW

➤ Proofread the following composition, and correct problems with fragments, run-on sentences, past tense forms, and past participles.

WHY I CAME TO COLLEGE

I started my senior year in high school, I realize that I only had one more year to decide what I would do after high school. I was very anxious about my future. By the end of that year. I had decide to go to college. There was three things that help me to decide for college.

First of all, I know that I wanted my life to be different from my father's life. My father had to quit school. When he were sixteen because his family need more money. He went to worked at a shoe factory. He hated the work, the money was good, his boss like him. Also, my dad did not had a high school diploma, he feel that he had to work in a factory. As a result, he had work at that same factory for thirty years. He told me that he did not cared what I decided

to do with my life. As long as I did not decided to work in a
factory. He think that I should get an education. So that I
would be able to find a better job than he had find.

Second, I did not knew what kind of job I want. All the
men in my family was factory workers, I did not know anything
about the lives of men who had other jobs. I was frighten by
the idea of getting a different kind of job. And discovering
that I hate the job. By going to college. I would be able to
waited a few more years. Before I had to decided on a job. I
also think that I would be able to learn more about other jobs
at college, I would have a better chance to find the right job
for me. After four years of college.

Finally, my high school counselor convince me that I was
smart enough. To go to college. My high school grades was
pretty good, I knew that my high school was a bad school, I
was afraid that I wasn't as intelligent as college students
had to be. My counselor had being to college, he think that I
could make it. After he tell me that several times. I was
convince that I had a chance to succeed in college.

Because of these three things, I decide to apply for
admission to a university. To my surprise, I was accept by
this university in March of my senior year. Then I was able to
relaxed and to enjoyed the rest of my senior year. Knowing
that I would be going to college the next fall.

## EXERCISE 11: EXTRA PROOFREADING PRACTICE

➤ Pick one of the pieces you wrote for a journal assignment in Part I of this
book. Proofread it, and correct any problems you may find with: past tense
verb forms, past participle markers, plural markers, subject-verb agreement,
fragments, or run-on sentences.

## EXERCISE 12: PROOFREADING TIP ON USING COMMAS WITH INTERRUPTING WORDS AND PHRASES

In Chapter 9, you learned that when you use semicolon connectors to combine two clauses into a good sentence, you should put a semicolon before the connector and a comma after the connector. In this exercise, we are going to consider sentences that are *exceptions* to this rule.

First, consider the following examples, which illustrate the rule you were taught in Chapter 9:

My sister wants to give our parents a surprise party on their wedding anniversary; however, my brother insists that our parents hate surprises.

The students have studied hard; therefore, they should have no difficulty passing the final examination.

My older sister wants to get married and have babies; on the other hand, my younger sister plans to become a lawyer.

Now consider these examples, which illustrate exceptions to the rule:

My sister wants to give our parents a surprise party on their wedding anniversary. My brother, however, insists that our parents hate surprises.

The students have studied hard. They should, therefore, have no difficulty passing the final examination.

My older sister wants to get married and have babies. My younger sister, on the other hand, plans to become a lawyer.

What makes the difference between the two groups of sentences? If you examine them carefully, you will discover that in the first group of sentences, the semicolon connectors are placed exactly between the two clauses. In other words, the semicolon connectors are placed *before* the second clause. However, in the second group, the connectors are placed not *before* the second clause but *in the middle of* the second clause. Because the connectors are in the middle of a clause, they are set off by commas on both sides. Here are some more examples that illustrate this rule:

Roberto plans to go to medical school. His brother, however, wants to become a commodities broker.

Sarah intends to make an A in chemistry. She will, therefore, study two hours every night for that class.

The teachers announced that they planned a strike. The mayor, subsequently, announced that he would help the school board find more funds.

To summarize what you've learned, we can use the following rule:

> *Rule 41:* Whenever a semicolon connector appears in the middle of a clause, it should be set off by commas on both sides.

➤ Use what you have learned in this exercise to proofread and correct the following sentences. If a sentence is correct, write "C" after it. The first sentence has been done for you.

1. Ray bought a new pair of jeans; however, he didn't need any.   *C*

2. Ann did that exercise carelessly. She, therefore, made a lot of embarrassing mistakes.

3. The television programs last night were terrible. I nevertheless watched them.

4. Cheryl is fascinated by people who have emotional troubles. She; therefore, wants to become a psychiatrist.

5. Jesse's girlfriend is very beautiful, moreover, she is quite intelligent.

6. That restaurant is very expensive. The food however tastes terrible.

7. Margaret plans to travel to Spain. She will; in addition, visit southern France.

8. Bill intends to spend a year studying in Germany. He will, as a result, get a chance to improve his mastery of German.

9. My husband is an excellent cook; moreover, he likes to clean house.

10. This exercise was tricky. I have; however, improved my ability to proofread for commas with semicolon connectors.

# TWELVE

## PROOFREADING THE SENTENCE: USING PRONOUNS CORRECTLY

**I**n this chapter, we will look at a kind of word that you already use quite naturally in spoken English but that may cause some difficulties in written English: the *pronoun*. Once again, nobody is likely to make an issue about your pronoun usage in the middle of a lively conversation. In a piece of written work, however, it is important to know how to choose the correct pronoun form, to make pronouns agree, and to avoid any problems with unclear pronoun reference.

### EXERCISE 1: CHOOSING CORRECT PRONOUN FORMS

Let's begin by considering some things that you already know about pronouns. In your earlier schooling, you were taught that pronouns "take the place of nouns," and that the following words are common English pronouns:

| I | we | you | he | she | it | they |
|---|----|-----|-----|-----|----|------|
| me | us | | him | her | | them |

In addition, you know when to use particular pronoun forms in most of the sentences that you write. For instance, you would never write the following sentences:

*Me* bought a blue sweater.
Mother bought *I* a new coat.

Instead, you would write these sentences:

*I* bought a blue sweater.
Mother bought *me* a new coat.

Similarly, you would never write sentences like these:

*Us* will see Bill this evening.
Bill will see *we* this evening.

However, you would write sentences like these:

*We* will see Bill this evening.
Bill will see *us* this evening.

So you already know a great deal about choosing the correct form of a pronoun.

In most cases, you naturally choose the correct pronoun form when you're writing. However, there is one situation in which many writers are unsure of which pronoun form to use. A tricky situation can arise when a pronoun is part of a *compound construction*—that is, where a noun and a pronoun are connected by the word *and*, or where two pronouns are connected by *and*. Here are some examples of sentences using pronouns in compound constructions:

*John and I* have dated for two months.
Gretchen said she saw *him and Elizabeth* doing the polka.
*He and she* seemed to be having a grand old time.
Apparently, the music drove *him and her* wild.
Gretchen wants to have a little talk with *Elizabeth and me*.

In sentences like these, the pronoun forms that you use when you talk may be different from the pronoun forms that you need to use when you are writing, so you may not know which pronoun form to use.

How then can you know when to use *I* or *me, she* or *her, he* or *him?* Fortunately you can use a very simple rule to help you choose the correct pronoun form. Whenever you have a compound construction, ask yourself which pronoun form you would use if the pronoun stood alone. For example, suppose you aren't sure whether to write:

You can go to the party with Bill and I.
  or
You can go to the party with Bill and me.

Just ask yourself which pronoun you would use if the pronoun stood alone. The correct answer would be, "You can go to the party with me," so you can figure out that you should write:

You can go to the party with Bill and me.

Suppose you are trying to decide whether to write:

Mario and she will get married on Saturday.
or
Mario and her will get married on Saturday.

If you use the rule, you will discover that the correct pronoun form is *she*. We can summarize what you have learned in the following rule:

> *Rule 42:* To discover which pronoun form to use when you have a pronoun in a *compound construction,* ask yourself which pronoun form you would use if the pronoun stood by itself.

Using Rule 42, proofread the following sentences, correcting any errors in pronoun form. If a sentence is correct, write "C" after it. The first sentence has been done for you.

1. Veronica and ~~her~~ she make straight A's.

2. Don and I will attend the wedding.

3. Helen told the story to Betty and I.

4. Let's keep this a secret between you and me.

5. Georgette and him want to double-date with Andre and me.

6. Donna and he are planning a surprise party for Shannon.

7. Him and me are going to take chemistry next term.

8. Tony Chen gave a ride to them and Mrs. Smith.

9. Sayed and me want to go with you and her.

10. How long will him and Mary study?

11. You can trust her and him.

12. Her and Imogene went shopping.

13. He and Noriko visited the Statue of Liberty.

14. The Robinsons and us are having dinner at an Italian restaurant on Saturday night.

15. Chang-li will treat you and I to dinner.


## EXERCISE 2: PRONOUN AGREEMENT

In Chapter 10 you learned that when you choose a particular subject, you have to make sure that you select the verb form that agrees with the subject. In this exercise, we're going to consider another kind of agreement problem that is particularly troublesome in written English—the problem of pronoun agreement.

First, let's consider what the term *pronoun agreement* means. Examine the following sentences:

*The boy* found the wallet, and *he* received a reward.
*The boys* found the wallet, and *they* received a reward.

In the first sentence, the writer uses the singular pronoun *he* because the pronoun refers to (means the same thing as) *the boy*. In the second sentence, the writer uses the plural pronoun *they* because the pronoun refers to (means the same thing as) the plural noun *the boys*. In other words, the singular pronoun *agrees with* the singular noun in the first sentence, and the plural pronoun *agrees with* the plural noun in the second.

For more examples, consider the following sentences:

*The girl* won the tournament, and *she* was congratulated by the mayor.
*The girls* won the tournament, and *they* were congratulated by the mayor.

In the first sentence, the singular pronoun *she* is used because it *agrees with* the singular noun *the girl*. In the second, the plural pronoun *they* is used because it *agrees with* the plural noun *the girls*.

This explanation may give you the feeling that pronoun agreement is so simple that you should never have a problem with it. Unfortunately, however, pronoun agreement can easily get you into difficulty because English is not always a perfectly logical language. In some sentences, singular nouns are used to talk about more than one person, and those sentences may cause problems with pronoun agreement. Consider the following example:

>    **A child needs a great deal of love.**

Here a singular noun, *child,* is being used to talk about *all* children. As a result, if you wrote *a child* to refer to children in general, it would be very easy to slip and use the plural pronoun *they.* The following sentences show this:

>    **A child needs a great deal of love. *They* need to feel secure when**
>        ***they* are very young.**

There is another reason why you may slip from singular to plural pronouns when you are using the singular noun, *child,* to talk about children in general. If you want to use a singular pronoun, what pronoun are you going to choose? Are you going to use a form of *he* or a form of *she*? Suppose you write this sentence:

>    **A child needs a great deal of love. *He* wants to feel secure when**
>        ***he*'s very young.**

You may feel that you have left out all the female children. On the other hand, suppose you write this sentence:

>    **A child needs a great deal of love. *She* wants to feel secure when**
>        ***she*'s very young.**

Then you have left out all the male children.

You may now be wondering if anyone can ever feel comfortable about knowing which singular pronoun to use, and you are right to wonder. Even professional writers are unsure of the best way to solve this problem.

One solution is to follow a rule that was followed until fairly recently: use the masculine pronoun forms (*he, his,* and *him*) to talk about people in general. Writers who use that rule produce sentences like these:

>    **A child needs a great deal of love. *He* wants to feel secure when**
>        ***he*'s very young.**

While such sentences are clear enough, few writers use them today because they are felt to be unfair to women.

Another possible solution is to use both a masculine (*he, him,* or *his*) and a feminine (*she* or *her*) pronoun with the connecting word *or.* For example:

> A child needs a great deal of love. *He or she* needs to feel secure
> when *he or she* is very young.

A third way of solving the problem is to change the noun to a plural form. After all, the following sentences mean the same thing:

> A child needs a great deal of love.
> Children need a great deal of love.

The writer who uses the plural noun form to talk about *children in general* will have no problems deciding which pronoun to use:

> Children need a great deal of love. *They* want to feel secure when
> *they* are very young.

Which of these three solutions should you use? Any one of the three approaches will help you avoid problems with pronoun agreement. All of the following sentences are acceptable in written English:

> A student has a right to expect that *his* professors will grade fairly.
> (This may be offensive to some readers, however.)
> A student has a right to expect that *his or her* professors will grade
> fairly.
> Students have a right to expect that *their* professors will grade
> fairly.

To summarize what you have learned, we can use the following rule:

---

*Rule 43:* Pronouns should always agree with the nouns they refer to. Singular pronouns should always refer to singular nouns, and plural pronouns should always refer to plural nouns.

---

➤ Use Rule 43 to proofread the following examples and correct any problems with pronoun agreement. If a sentence is correct, write "C" after it. The first sentence has been done for you.

1. ~~A good writer spends~~ Good writers spend time rewriting because they want their ideas to be understood.

2. A doctor knows that people's lives are in his or her hands.

3. A politician should be honest. They should never consider taking bribes.

4. A student who wants an education attends classes regularly. He only misses classes when he is sick.

5. Philosophers spend their lives searching for truth.

6. A poet truly understands how to use language. They have the power to use words to capture emotions.

7. A good supervisor knows how to help his or her subordinates perform exceptionally well.

8. A child is disturbed by the thought of divorce. They are afraid that if their parents stop loving one another, then perhaps their parents can stop loving them.

9. A good teacher wants his students to learn.

10. A professional musician practices for several hours every day. They know that practice makes perfect.

11. A person who watches soap operas all day long may begin to believe that his life is very boring.

12. Students majoring in pre-law discover that they must worry about pronoun agreement and subject-verb agreement because they must understand grammar in order to understand legal language.

13. Life becomes difficult when an individual discovers that they cannot trust their closest friend.

14. If you ask the chief executive officer of a corporation what was the most important thing they learned in college, they will tell you that the most important thing they learned was how to think critically.

15. Novelists are people who have learned how to turn their life experiences into stories that other people are interested in reading.

# EXERCISE 3: SPECIAL AGREEMENT PROBLEMS WITH THE WORDS *ANYONE, EVERYONE,* AND *NO ONE*

As you learned in Exercise 2, in English we sometimes use nouns that are singular when we are talking about people in general. In this exercise, we will consider a special group of singular words that are often used to talk about people in general. These special words, sometimes called *indefinite pronouns,* are *anyone, everyone,* and *no one.*

Because these special words are used to talk about people in general, we often use plural pronouns to refer to these words in spoken English. The following sentences show this:

Anyone can learn to swim if *they* really want to.
Everyone has *their* own way of doing things.
No one in *their* right mind would want to live in Siberia.

However, because indefinite pronouns are singular words, the careful writer will use singular pronouns. So, when you use these indefinites in written English, be sure that you use singular pronouns.

There are two ways to rewrite the above sentences. A traditional way is to use the masculine pronoun:

Anyone can learn to swim if *he* really wants to.
Everyone has *his* own way of doing things.
No one in *his* right mind would want to live in Siberia.

However, as we saw in the last exercise, this solution is offensive to many readers today, since it seems to ignore the female half of the population. The other way is to use both the masculine and feminine pronouns with the connecting word *or:*

Anyone can learn to swim if *he or she* really wants to.
Everyone has *his or her* own way of doing things.
No one in *his or her* right mind would want to live in Siberia.

The following rule summarizes what we have learned:

*Rule 44:* For agreement with the words *anyone, everyone,* and *no one,* use singular pronouns in written English.

➤ Use Rule 44 to proofread and correct the following sentences. If a sentence is correct, write "C" after it. The first sentence has been done for you.

1. Anyone who wants an A in English should proofread his or her compositions carefully.  *C*

2. No one wants other people to hate them.

3. Everyone has a right to his or her own opinion.

4. Anyone can learn the rules for pronoun agreement if they want to.

5. Everyone feels, at some point in his life, that he has been misunderstood.

6. Anyone can learn to appreciate classical music if he or she likes jazz.

7. No one can like the taste of jalapeño peppers the first time he tries them.

8. Everyone wants to find that special person who will accept them completely.

9. Everyone needs to find some time in the week when they can relax and forget about school or work.

10. No one would rent an apartment in a slum building if they could afford to pay for better housing.

## EXERCISE 4: PROBLEMS WITH UNCLEAR PRONOUN REFERENCE

In this exercise, we will consider another kind of proofreading problem with pronouns: the problem of *unclear pronoun reference*.

In order to understand this problem, we first need to consider what the term *pronoun reference* means. Examine the following pairs of sentences:

Martin stared at the painting for a long time. *It* reminded *him* of the small town where *he* grew up.

Mrs. Friedman told the children about *her* life in the Soviet Union. *They* were amazed to learn about all the things that had happened to *her*.

In these pairs of sentences, you have no difficulty figuring out what the pronouns mean. In the first pair, the pronoun *it* means *the painting,* and the pronouns *him* and *he* mean *Martin.* To use slightly different words, the pronoun *it* refers to *the painting,* and the pronouns *him* and *he* refer to *Martin.* Similarly, in the second pair, the pronoun *her* refers to *Mrs. Friedman,* and the pronoun *they* refers to *the children.* So, when people talk about *pronoun reference,* they are simply talking about the noun that a particular pronoun refers to.

So far we have looked at sentences that make it easy for you to discover what nouns the pronouns refer to, but there are other sentences in which you may find it difficult to discover what the pronouns refer to. The following pairs of sentences show this:

> The car knocked over the fence. He was very angry.
> This college should offer courses in Japanese. They will have many
>      job opportunities in the business world.
> Sherman thought Eileen looked beautiful that night, but Rachel
>      was his date. Finally, he asked her to dance.

In the first sentence, it is difficult to discover who the angry person is: The driver of the car? The owner of the fence? Someone else? The sentence simply doesn't tell you. In the second example, does the writer mean to say that students who take courses in Japanese will find many job opportunities, or that people in business will have many opportunities to offer them? And in the third example, it's hard to decide whether Sherman asked Eileen or Rachel to dance. In other words, in each case, the writer has produced an *unclear pronoun reference.*

When use of a pronoun may obscure your meaning, it is probably better not to use the pronoun. Notice how easy it is to understand these examples:

> The car ran into the fence, and the driver got very angry.
> This college should offer courses in Japanese. Students who know
>      Japanese will have many job opportunities in business.
> Sherman thought Eileen looked beautiful that night, but Rachel
>      was his date. Finally, he asked Rachel to dance.

We can summarize what we have discussed so far with the following rule:

> *Rule 45:* Check to make sure that your reader will be able
>      to find the noun that a pronoun refers to. If the reference
>      is unclear, then use a specific noun rather than an unclear
>      pronoun.

➤ Using Rule 45, proofread the following, and correct any problems with unclear pronoun reference. If a sentence or pair of sentences is correct, write "C" after it. The first sentence has been done for you.

1. The car was heading toward a huge semi-truck. ~~It~~ *The truck* seemed to be out of control.

2. Mr. Johnson bought a digital clock. He paid only thirty dollars for it.

3. Unemployment is a terrible problem in this state, because they lose their jobs and are unable to find any others.

4. Books are windows that let us see the world. They introduce us to countries that we can't afford to visit.

5. When Connie and Steve met with the lawyer, he asked a lot of questions.

6. The cafeteria here should be improved. They pay $3.50 for a hamburger, and it tastes horrible.

7. My aunt likes classical music more than my uncle does. All day at the office, she has her radio tuned to the classical music station.

8. There were only seven students in the class. They learned a great deal because the teacher had time for individual instruction.

9. Hank asked Paul whether he had caused the accident.

10. Some people enjoy living in small towns. They like the peace, the quiet, and the sense of community.

11. Guns n' Roses are a good band, but I think he has a lot of prejudiced attitudes.

12. Between Guns n' Roses and Public Enemy, I like them more.

## EXERCISE 5: PROOFREADING FOR PRONOUN PROBLEMS

➤ Proofread the following composition looking for problems with pronouns. The first correction has been made for you.

## THE LIFE OF A TEENAGER

*Teenagers*
~~A teenager~~ today cannot believe that their parents ever
felt anything similar to what they feel. But my husband and
me were teenagers in the 1960s, and we think the life of a
teenager today is really quite similar to the life of a
teenager in the 1960s in many ways.

There are some differences. They grow up in families
that are very different from what my generation experienced.
In the sixties, my husband and me knew a few teenagers whose
parents had been divorced, but we didn't know many. They
lived with both their parents, and they assumed their parents
would stay together until one died. Today they don't assume
that their parents will live together until death. In fact,
my children are unusual because their two parents actually
live together and have only been married once. Today, the
typical teenager either has only one parent living with them,
or they have one or two stepparents to deal with. Moreover,
there are a few teenagers whose parents have been married and
divorced two or three times. As a result, any teenager in a
two-parent home worries that his or her parents will someday
get divorced. So no teenager in the 1990s assumes they can
depend on their parents the way teenagers did in my day.

For another difference, the role of women has changed. A
teenaged girl in the 1960s didn't worry about choosing a
career. They were supposed to become wives and mothers. If a
woman planned to go to college, her main reason for going was
to find a husband who would support she and her children.
They assumed they would never have to get a job. They would be
full-time wives and mothers. Today they worry about choosing
a career. They assume that a woman is supposed to have a

career. No one plans to stay home and take care of their
children all day long, so they plan to go to college in order
to prepare themselves for a good job. A teenaged girl worries
as much as a teenaged boy does about choosing a field that
will permit them to make money. So teenagers today do have to
worry about a few things that didn't worry my friends and I in
the 1960s.

Nevertheless, there are a lot of similarities. For one
thing, a teenager always worries a great deal about the way
they look. Clothes are the most important thing on earth. In
the 1960s, a teenaged girl thought that the world would come
to an end if her parents didn't let her wear miniskirts
because everyone had to have clothes like their friends had.
A teenaged boy had to wear Levis and flannel shirts, or
everyone would think he was weird. Today a teenager thinks
that the world will come to an end if they don't have whatever
length of sweater is in style this year and several pairs of
designer jeans because anyone who wants to be popular has to
dress the way their friends dress. Also, hair is always a
major trauma for a teenager. In the 1960s teenaged boys and
girls fought for the right to wear long hair. Anyone who
wanted to be popular had to have their hair at least
shoulder-length. For most of the 1980s, they wanted their
hair short. Now they want it long again. No matter what the
current style, a teenager must always look like their
friends.

For another similarity, a teenager always tries to drive
their parents crazy. They want to have their own kind of
music which must be very different from the music their
parents like so their parents will get upset. In the 1960s
teenagers listened to the Beatles and the Rolling Stones, and

they were really very pleased when their parents complained
about the terrible music. In the 1990s a teenager listens to
heavy metal and rap music records that adults think no person
in their right mind would listen to, and the teenager today
is very happy when his or her parents complain about the
horrible noise. Finally, a teenager always wants to spend
hours talking on the telephone because they know that sooner
or later, their parents will complain. In the 1960s me and my
friends would spend hours every night talking on the
telephone, waiting for the moment when our parents would yell
at us to get off the phone and do our homework. My teenaged
children do the same thing now.

In summary, life for a teenager today is more similar to
the life of a teenager in the 1960s than they think. Anyone
who was a teenager in the 1960s can understand many of their
children's feelings about the life of a teenager.

## EXERCISE 6: PROOFREADING REVIEW

➤ Proofread the following composition for problems with fragments, run-ons,
plural markers, subject-verb agreement, *-ed* endings, and pronouns.

### PEOPLE AND THEIR PETS

One night me and my friends had a long discussion about
what makes a person buy a particular pet. Since then, I have
thought a lot about this subject, and I have discovered that
they tell a lot about their view of animals by the pets they
choose. In fact, I have decide that I can classify pet owners
into four group.

The first group includes the fish owners. Anyone who belongs in this category feel that animals should never be allowed to disturbed his life. A fish owner don't want a pet that requires much attention, they choose a fish because it needs so little from them. Just some food and every so often a clean tank. In addition, a fish owner wants a pet that will never make the house dirty. They choose a pet that will never touch their furniture or anything else in the house except the fish tank. For another characteristic. A fish owner wants peace and quiet, they choose an animal that will never make any noise. Finally, a fish owner doesn't want much from an animal. All he wants is something that he can look at. Whenever he feels like it. So the fish owner keeps his pet at a distance.

The second kind of pet owner is the bird person. Anyone in this group is willing to let their pet disturb their life occasionally. As long as the pet don't cause too much trouble. A bird owner does not demand peace and quiet from a pet. They enjoy the chattering or singing of the bird, they don't even mind if the bird wake them up at 5:00 A.M. with a song. They don't mind because they can always put a cover over the bird cage. When they don't want to hear any noise. For another characteristic, the bird owner is willing to let his pet out of the cage so that it can fly freely around the house and even make an occasional mess; however, the bird owner can put the bird back in the cage when he or she doesn't want to bother with the pet. Finally, a bird owner knows that bird don't require much attention. Just food, water, and a clean cage. As a result, the bird owner can give his pet as much attention or as little attention as they feel like giving. In summary, a bird person feel that an animal can be

allow to touch a person's life as long as the owner can
control the amount of contact.

Next, the cat lover. Cat lovers are willing to let their
pets disturb their lives at any time. Cats are permit to roam
freely through the house leaving cat hair on all the chair.
And even jumping up on the table when the owner is eating. Cat
lovers are willing to let their cats do these things because
they get affection from their cats. The cat lover is happy
when their cat rubs against their leg and purrs contentedly.
Also, cat owners can give a lot of affection to their cats.
They enjoy having their cat jump up on their lap to be petted
while they're watching television. However, the cat person
knows that cats are very independent. The cat person doesn't
have to be home at a certain time each day to walk the cat, so
the person who owns a cat. Doesn't feel that his life is
control by his pet. Also, there are time when cats want to be
left alone. When those times come, the cat lover can have
some freedom from his pet. In short, a cat person wants an
animal that will touch his or her life a lot. But will also be
very independent.

The fourth kind of pet owner is the dog lover. They want
to give a lot of love to an animal, they choose a pet that
likes a lot of love and affection. A dog needs a lot of love.
They are willing to be petted at any time. A dog also needs a
lot of attention. They have to be walked at various times
during the day, the dog person must schedule his life around
the life of his pet. The dog person is willing to do all these
things because they know that dog will give a great deal in
return. A dog will learn to do tricks and play games. In order
to please his or her master. Dogs will also protect their
owners by barking whenever strangers come around. So a dog

lover wants to give a lot of love to their pet and receive a
lot of love in return.

In conclusion, people choose different pets because
different people has different views on how much animal
should be allowed to disturb their lives. Some people want to
be disturb a lot, some people don't want to be disturbed at
all. Others are somewhere in between.

## EXERCISE 7: EXTRA PROOFREADING PRACTICE

➤ Pick one of the pieces you wrote for a journal assignment in Part I of this
book. Proofread it, and correct any problems you may find with: pronoun
use, past tense verb forms, past participle markers, plural markers, subject-
verb agreement, fragments, or run-on sentences.

## EXERCISE 8: PROOFREADING TIP ON USING
## COMMAS WITH RELATIVE PRONOUNS

In Chapter 9, you learned that the rule that tells you when to use commas
with relative pronoun constructions is very complex. In this exercise, we will
consider this particular comma rule.

Let's begin by examining the following sentences:

A man who has a good job will make a good husband.
A city which has bad public transportation is a poor place to live.
A student who misses lots of classes will probably make bad
grades.
A lake which is polluted is a dangerous place to go swimming.
Bill Jones, who has a good job, will make a good husband.
Los Angeles, which has bad public transportation, is a poor place
to live.
Margie Smith, who misses lots of classes, will probably make bad
grades.
Lake Montgomery, which is polluted, is a dangerous place to go
swimming.

Notice that there are no commas in the first four sentences, but there are commas in the second four. What makes the difference? To answer this question, we need to examine the sentences carefully.

In the first four sentences, if you leave out the relative pronoun constructions, the meaning of the sentences will change dramatically. For example:

A man will make a good husband.
A city is a poor place to live.
A student will probably make bad grades.
A lake is a dangerous place to go swimming.

However, if you leave out the relative pronoun constructions in the last four sentences, the meaning of the sentences will not change dramatically. The following sentences illustrate this:

Bill Jones will make a good husband.
Los Angeles is a poor place to live.
Margie Smith will probably make bad grades.
Lake Montgomery is a dangerous place to go swimming.

You may have concluded that when the meaning *changes dramatically,* you do *not* use commas—but when the meaning *does not change dramatically,* you *do* use commas. Here are some more sentences for you to consider:

My brother will marry any woman who likes football.
My brother will marry Liz Anderson, who likes football.

That professor will give an A to any student who works hard.
That professor will give an A to George Matthews, who works hard.

David refuses to go out with women who smoke.
David refuses to go out with Rosemary Lincoln, who smokes.

In these examples, as in those above, commas are *not* used if the meaning changes dramatically when you remove the relative clause. Commas *are* used if the meaning does not change dramatically if you remove the relative clause.

To summarize what you have learned, use the following rule:

> *Rule 46:* If the meaning of the sentence will change dramatically when you leave out the relative pronoun construction, then you never use commas to set off the construction. If the meaning will not change dramatically when you leave out the relative pronoun construction, then you do use commas to set off the construction.

➤ Use what you have learned in this exercise to proofread and correct the following sentences. If a sentence is correct, write "C" after it. The first sentence has been done for you.

1. Students who read a lot tend to improve their writing quickly.　*C*

2. Bob Martin who studies three hours every night makes straight A's.

3. Greta plans to marry Dr. Dixon, who is a heart surgeon at Cedars Memorial Hospital.

4. Writers, who never proofread, make lots of careless mistakes.

5. The city of New York which almost went bankrupt has improved its credit rating.

6. Mohammed is willing to marry any woman who has lots of money.

7. My professor comes from Oak Park which is a suburb of Dallas.

8. A woman who refuses to get a job should not receive welfare.

9. Mr. Kim, who is my landlord, owns four apartment buildings.

10. Bob and Mary like movies that have happy endings.

11. Mr. and Mrs. Chen need an apartment which has three bedrooms.

12. A teacher, who doesn't prepare for class, should be fired.

13. Never trust any person who is always cheerful.

14. People, who litter the parks, should be forced to spend their Saturdays cleaning parks.

15. People who are in love are very lucky.

# ANSWERS TO SELECTED EXERCISES

## ANSWERS TO SENTENCE-COMBINING EXERCISES IN PART I

Here are sample answers for some of the sentence-combining exercises in Part I of this book. There are sample combinations given for each of the first two exercises in every Sentence-Combining Practice. Then, a suggested answer is given for the first few sentences in every "Putting It Together" exercise. Remember that sentences can often be combined in many different ways, and that these are just a few of the possible combinations.

### CHAPTER 1

**5 Sentence Combining in Written English: Relative Pronouns (p. 15)**

1. I met a girl who lives on the fourth floor of my building.
   I met a girl that lives on the fourth floor of my building.
2. The woman who is a doctor is the mother of four.
   The woman that is a doctor is the mother of four.

**6 Sentence Combining: Putting It Together (p. 23)**

1–8. Everyone has one special place that they really like. My favorite spot is a campground that is in Wisconsin on the shores of Lake Michigan. It has lots of campsites that are not close together, so my friends and I don't feel surrounded by people.

### CHAPTER 2

**5 Sentence Combining in Written English: Chronological Order (p. 34)**

1. Dennis dusted the furniture before he vacuumed the carpet.
   After Dennis dusted the furniture, he vacuumed the carpet.
2. Vivian was studying her English while Sheila watched television.
   As Vivian was studying her English, Sheila watched television.

**6 Sentence Combining: Putting It Together (p. 40)**

1–8. When I was a sophomore in college, I had a strange experience in a linguistics class. One morning the room was filled with sleepy students when the professor, who was very young, walked into the room. When he slammed his books on the desk, the students jumped.

### CHAPTER 3

**5 Sentence Combining in Written English: Comparison and Contrast (p. 51)**

1. Rita likes classical music; however, her sister prefers rock music.
   Rita likes classical music, but her sister prefers rock music.
2. Although his brother was a high school dropout, Jeremy plans to go to medical school.
   Jeremy plans to go to medical school; however, his brother was a high school dropout.

**6 Sentence Combining: Putting It Together (p. 57)**

1–7. Because my mother doesn't know much about baseball and football, she thinks the two sports are very similar. However, I have played both sports, so I know the two sports are really very different.

   (First, let's look at the similarities.) Baseball and football are played outdoors, so the weather can be very important.

### CHAPTER 4

**5 Sentence Combining in Written English: Generalizations and Examples (p. 71)**

1. The game of bridge helps you improve your powers of concentration; for example, you must pay attention to every card that is played so that you can outsmart your opponents.

2. Jogging is good for your cardiovascular system. For example, when you run for thirty minutes, your heart muscles get stronger as the heart works to pump blood to all parts of your body.

### 6   Sentence Combining: Putting It Together (p. 76)

1–7. Every Saturday night, my sister and brother-in-law rent a movie on videotape, because they want to save money and videotapes are inexpensive. Because my wife and I want to save money, sometimes we rent videotapes on weekends, but once a month we go out to a movie at a budget theater.

### CHAPTER 5

### 5   Sentence Combining in Written English: Appositive Constructions (p. 95)

1. I just finished *Bury My Heart at Wounded Knee,* a history of Native Americans.

2. Stephanie wants to major in geology, the study of the earth's crust.

### 6   Sentence Combining: Putting It Together (p. 99)

1–8. I have lived in many apartment buildings and have had many neighbors. From my experiences, I have concluded that there are three kinds of neighbors: the neighbor from hell, the mystery neighbor, and the good neighbor.

   Neighbors from hell, who make your life a constant nightmare, are the worst kind of neighbor you can have.

### CHAPTER 6

### 5   Sentence Combining in Written English: Cause-and-Effect Sentences (p. 115)

1. Because I have too much homework, I can't go to the movie tonight.
   I have too much homework; therefore I can't go to the movie tonight.

2. My car is falling apart, so I must buy a new one.
   Because my car is falling apart, I must buy a new one.

### 6   Sentence Combining: Putting It Together (p. 119)

1–12. I wish I lived in an ideal world, a perfect place filled with people that are really nice. But I live in the real world, an imperfect place with people that are not very nice. There's one person in particular who constantly gets on my nerves. That person is Bertha, my sister-in-law.

## ANSWERS TO EXERCISES IN PART II

Here are sample answers for some of the exercises in Part II of this book. Answers are provided for the *first half* of all exercise sets that are made up of numbered sentences. There are no answers given for exercises that ask you to proofread complete compositions.

### CHAPTER 7

### Exercise 2   Recognizing Verbs (p. 128)

2. seems, 3. locked, 4. drives, 5. will taste, 6. answered, 7. makes, 8. forgot, 9. has, 10. went

### Exercise 3   More on Verbs: Auxiliary Verbs (p. 131)

2. grew, 3. has been, 4. Did . . . study, 5. has disappeared, 6. must speak, 7. sounds, 8. is, 9. talks, 10. Will . . . win

### Exercise 4   Recognizing Subjects (p. 134)

2. My radio and my stereo were, 3. The president should lead, 4. did you come, 5. Santa Claus gave, 6. The children are playing,

7. (Seth) has . . . wanted, 8. (The roses) need, 9. (My car) uses, 10. (The pink panther) chased

## CHAPTER 8

### Exercise 1   Good Sentences versus Fragments (p. 138)

Many corrections of the fragments are possible. The following are suggested answers only.

2. C
3. The girl in the brown sweater is my sister.
4. C
5. The deer ran over the river and through the woods.
6. She saw the man with the cocker spaniel.
7. I was pushing my car to Halsted.
8. C

17. C
18. A black cat with white tips on its ears climbed up on the fence.
19. You can have the book from now until the end of the term.
20. A beautiful woman with curly black hair asked Herman for a date.
21. My baby cried all night long, so I am very tired this morning.

### Exercise 2   Fragment Problems with Sentence Connectors (p. 141)

2. Because the smoke burned the firemen's eyes, they had to leave the building.
3. C
4. C
5. Although Bill hates biology, he intends to get an A in it.
6. C
7. Gloria screamed when she saw a snake.
8. C
9. When the baseball players went on strike, Dave became interested in soccer.
10. C

### Exercise 3   Fragment Problems with Relative Pronouns (p. 144)

2. C
3. C

4. Sue grew up in Cape Girardeau, which is a small town in Missouri.
5. (Fragment; many correct answers possible)

### Exercise 4   Real Verbs versus False Verbs (p. 145)

2. F, 3. F, 4. C, 5. F, 6. F, 7. F, 8. C

### Exercise 5   Commands versus Fragments (p. 148)

Many corrections of the fragments are possible. The following are suggested answers only.

2. C
3. He wants to drop the course.
4. The teacher is angry.
5. C

### Exercise 6   Reviewing Good Sentences versus Fragments (p. 149)

Many corrections of the fragments are possible. The following are suggested answers only.

2. C
3. The student trying to find the cafeteria is hungry enough to eat stale potato chips.
4. C
5. Mrs. Davis is on vacation and won't be back for two weeks.
6. C
7. The professor is looking for a piece of chalk.
8. If money can't buy happiness, why do so many people want money?
9. The woman with a purple coat and a brown plaid scarf is Bob's wife.
10. The man failed his driver's test and is afraid to try again.
11. C
12. Don't count your chickens until they're hatched.
13. Louisa is looking for a turquoise dress which has a long skirt.
14. No one ever listens to him, because his stories are very boring.
15. The guy driving the red Cadillac used to date my sister.

### Exercise 8 Proofreading Tip on Using Commas with Introductory Phrases (p. 152)

2. lakeshore,; 3. C; 4. meeting,; 5. C; 6. lake,

## CHAPTER 9

### Exercise 1 Good Sentences versus Run-ons: Using Comma Connectors (p. 155)

Some run-ons may be correctable in more than one way. The following are suggested answers.

2. Anthony found an apartment, but it was very expensive.
3. Elizabeth spends money foolishly, so she is always broke.
4. C
5. Barbara baked a cake, and Sue baked a pie.
6. Tony's wife is angry with him, and she won't cook his meals.
7. His stories are boring, so no one ever listens to him.
8. C

### Exercise 2 Good Sentences versus Run-ons: Using Two-place Connectors (p. 158)

Some run-ons may be correctable in more than one way. The following are suggested answers.

2. I need to buy a new coat, because mine is falling apart.
3. C
4. Walter cooked dinner while his wife read the newspaper.
5. C
6. C
7. C
8. Although I didn't study for the test, I made an A.

### Exercise 3 Good Sentences with Semicolon Connectors (p. 159)

Some run-ons may be correctable in more than one way. The following are suggested answers.

2. C
3. Howard is very intelligent; however, he doesn't believe it.

4. This room doesn't have enough chairs; however, it is the only one available.
5. C

### Exercise 4 Good Sentences with Relative Pronouns (p. 161)

2. C
3. Gladys is going out with Dr. Gonzalez, who owns a Mercedes-Benz.
4. They were searching for the dog that had a broken leg.
5. Bill is dating Gloria Marshall, who has expensive tastes.
6. C

### Exercise 5 Reviewing Good Sentences versus Run-ons (p. 162)

Some run-ons may be correctable in more than one way. The following are suggested answers.

2. The television programs last night were terrible, so I read a good book.
3. C
4. C
5. Ray bought a new pair of jeans, although he didn't need any.
6. If you do this exercise too rapidly, you will make a lot of mistakes.
7. Sue works carelessly; therefore, she makes a lot of foolish mistakes.
8. C
9. When James Bond entered the room, he saw a beautiful woman.
10. C

### Exercise 6 Long Sentences versus Run-ons (p. 164)

Some run-ons may be correctable in more than one way. The following are suggested answers.

2. My girlfriend hates football and loves movies, but I love football and hate movies.
3. C
4. Driving a car is very expensive, but no buses run close to my house, so I have to drive to school.
5. Greg is a good student who studies four hours every night, but Rodney is a poor student who never studies.

**Exercise 10 Proofreading Tip on When Not to Use Commas (p. 170)**

2. table,; 3. (delete comma); 4. C; 5. C;
6. Vegas,; 7. him,; 8. (delete comma)

## CHAPTER 10

**Exercise 1 Plural Markers (p. 172)**

2. C, 3. guards . . . hours, 4. students, 5. C /
12. students, 13. fruit, 14. C, 15. movie

### Exercise 2 Subject-Verb Agreement with Present Tense Verbs (p. 176)

2. C, 3. C, 4. C, 5. wants / 12. C, 13. C,
14. buys, 15. C, 16. chases, 17. bores,
18. knows / 27. C, 28. C, 29. C, 30. loves,
31. notice, 32. needs, 33. visit, 34. play, 35. C,
36. teach, 37. C, 38. C

### Exercise 3 Subject-Verb Agreement with Helping Verbs (p. 180)

2. C, 3. doesn't, 4. C, 5. do, 6. has, 7. Do,
8. doesn't, 9. C, 10. C, 11. types, 12. C,
13. live / 27. has, 28. C, 29. C, 30. are,
31. are, 32. C, 33. is, 34. pretend, 35. Are /
47. C, 48. meet, 49. may, 50. C

### Exercise 4 Subject-Verb Agreement with Compound Verbs (p. 185)

2. C, 3. practices, sings; 4. run, pass, speed;
5. prepares, grades; 6. C; 7. drinks; 8. C;
9. sleeps; 10. C

### Exercise 5 Special Problems with *here* and *there* (p. 186)

2. are, 3. C, 4. have, 5. C, 6. C, 7. are,
8. seems

### Exercise 6 Agreement with Verbs Separated from Their Subjects (p. 188)

2. C, 3. C, 4. want, 5. C, 6. C

### Exercise 7 Agreement in Two-Clause Sentences (p. 190)

2. loves, 3. doesn't, 4. C, 5. weighs, 6. get,
7. believe, 8. C, 9. understands, 10. C

**Exercise 11 Proofreading Tip on Using Commas with Compound Constructions (p. 197)**

2. broccoli, cauliflower,; 3. C; 4. sings,; 5. C;
6. measles, mumps,

## CHAPTER 11

**Exercise 1 Simple Past Tense and Regular Verbs (p. 200)**

2. C, 3. listened, 4. C, 5. husband wanted,
6. C, 7. jumped, 8. walked, 9. attended,
10. asked / 22. learn, 23. tried, 24. sailed,
25. C, 26. decided, 27. approve . . . refused,
28. C

### Exercise 2 The Verb *do* and the Past Tense (p. 203)

2. C, 3. C, 4. learn . . . wanted . . . learn,
5. cross, 6. C, 7. visit, 8. C

### Exercise 3 The Verb *be* and the Past Tense (p. 204)

2. C, 3. C, 4. was, 5. C, 6. C / 14. C, 15. C,
16. were, 17. C, 18. were, 19. C, 20. were /
29. C, 30. was, 31. were, 32. were

### Exercise 4 Past Tense Forms of Some Common Irregular Verbs (p. 208)

2. C, 3. found, 4. C, 5. ate, 6. C, 7. C,
8. came, 9. forgot, 10. C, 11. bring, 12. C,
13. find / 26. knew, 27. C, 28. have, 29. C,
30. C, 31. gave, 32. left, 33. hear, 34. C,
35. met, 36. kept, 37. go, 38. C / 51. tell,
52. C, 53. took, 54. think . . . said, 55. C,
56. sought, 57. C, 58. said, 59. C, 60. wrote,
61. C, 62. run, 63. C

### Exercise 5 Problems with Tense Agreement (p. 213)

2. became, 3. C, 4. C, 5. heard, 6. walked,
7. dented, 8. C, 9. C, 10. C

### Exercise 6 The Past Participle: The Helping Verb *have* and the *-ed* Verb Form (p. 216)

2. C, 3. C, 4. bombed, 5. studied, 6. C, 7. destroyed, 8. discovered, 9. C, 10. arranged

256

## Exercise 7 The Past Participle: The Helping Verb *be* and the *-ed* Verb Form (p. 217)

2. C, 3. questioned, 4. C, 5. required, 6. defeated, 7. bored, 8. destroyed, 9. C, 10. C

## Exercise 8 Past Participles for Some Common Irregular Verbs (p. 220)

2. C, 3. forgotten, 4. C, 5. C, 6. fallen, 7. C, 8. brought, 9. come, 10. C, 11. chosen, 12. eaten, 13. C / 26. C, 27. C, 28. C, 29. made, 30. grown, 31. gone, 32. C, 33. met, 34. put, 35. C, 36. has not had, 37. C, 38. C / 51. told, 52. written, 53. C, 54. C, 55. C, 56. C, 57. spoken, 58. understood, 59. C, 60. C, 61. thought, 62. C, 63. C

## Exercise 12 Proofreading Tip on Using Commas with Interrupting Words and Phrases (p. 229)

2. C; 3. I, nevertheless,; 4. She, therefore,; 5. beautiful; moreover,

## CHAPTER 12

### Exercise 1 Choosing Correct Pronoun Forms (p. 231)

2. C, 3. Betty and me, 4. C, 5. Georgette and he, 6. C, 7. He and I, 8. C

### Exercise 2 Pronoun Agreement (p. 234)

Some sentences may be corrected in more than one way. The following are suggested corrections only.

2. C

3. A politician should be honest and should never consider taking bribes.

4. Students who want an education attend classes regularly. They only miss classes when they are sick.

5. C

6. Poets truly understand how to use language. They have the power . . .

7. C

8. Children are disturbed by the thought of divorce . . .

### Exercise 3 Special Agreement Problems with the Words *anyone,* *everyone,* and *no one* (p. 238)

2. . . . to hate him or her, 3. C, 4. . . . if he or she wants to, 5. C (but possibly offensive)

### Exercise 4 Problems with Unclear Pronoun Reference (p. 239)

Some sentences may be corrected in more than one way. The following are suggested corrections only.

2. C, 3. . . . because people lose their jobs . . . , 4. C, 5. . . . Steve (or "the lawyer") asked a lot of questions, 6. . . . Students pay $3.50 . . .

### Exercise 8 Proofreading Tip on Using Commas with Relative Pronouns (p. 247)

2. Bob Martin, who studies three hours every night, makes . . . , 3. C, 4. Writers who never proofread make . . . , 5. . . . New York, which almost went bankrupt, has improved . . . , 6. C, 7. . . . Oak Park, which is a suburb . . . , 8. C

# INDEX

ISBN 978-1-58316-066-4